hi-fashion
sewing and
tailoring...

Illustrations by
Nancy T. Bunce

hi-fashion
sewing and tailoring

helen s. jones

PARLIAMENT PUBLISHERS
1848 West 2300 South
Salt Lake City, Utah

5th Printing, 1974

Printed in the United States of America

LITHOGRAPHED IN U.S.A. BY

PUBLISHERS PRESS
SALT LAKE CITY UTAH

Dedicated to my mother -- Florence Jones Peck.

Her creativity and sewing flair stimulated my

interest in sewing and showed me that sewing is

fun and exciting!

Contents

Preface

There's one in every community -- a seamstress who looks like she stepped from the pages of our leading fashion magazines. How does she do it -- without a "home-made" look? She has undoubtedly learned the knack of selecting a style and fabric that enhances her figure. And, she knows that the correct shaping fabrics, notions, trims, finishing touches and techniques will enable her to create a "masterpiece" that looks like the picture on the pattern envelope.

WHAT'LL I DO NOW?

Preface

While visiting a small city library recently, this sign on a bulletin board caught my attention. It suggested: "Don't spend time reading any book--read only great books". How true in sewing! Time is your most priceless possession, so create "great" looking and fitting garments rather than just another one!

This book is designed to help you create a "great looking wardrobe". I have included many professional tips and time-saving factory shortcuts which will be valuable in sewing simple or detailed garments. Much of the information answers questions which women have asked me while conducting sewing workshops and clinics during the past three years. Information is geared to "today's fibers, fabrics and finishes".

To help you construct professional looking suits and coats, there are two sections on tailoring--custom and speed. In "Custom Tailoring" much detail work is done by hand. Due to the amount of hand work and time involved, these techniques are suggested for your best quality woolens, silks, cashmeres, etc. The "Speed Tailoring" techniques can be used with all types of fabrics. They are designed for you gals who enjoy creating professional looking garments in the least amount of time. Machine stitching replaces most hand work.

Helen Jones

Fashion Designer Names
... often mispronounced ...

Balenciaga
(Bah-lawN-see-ah'gah)

Jacques Heim
(Zhahk Em)

Madame Grès
(Gray)

Patou
(Paa-too')

Marc Bohan
(Mark Bo-hoN')

house of Lanvin
(LaaN-vaaN')

Castillo
(Kah-stee'yoh)

pierre Cardin
(Pyehr Kahr-daaN')

Simonetta ~ Fabiani
(See-moh-net' tah;
Fah-bee-ah'nee)

guy Laroche
(Ghee Lah-rohsh)

yves St. Laurent
(Eve SaaN Lor-awN')

hubert de Givenchy
(Oo-behr' duh Jee-vawN-shee')

Flatter the Figure

Ever catch yourself saying -- "I don't have a thing to wear"?

This shouldn't happen if you have planned a wardrobe geared to your activities and your community. Naturally, you don't want your clothing to duplicate your neighbors', but check the trends-- formal, tailored, dressy, casual, or sporty??

Dress so you look well in your clothing. When selecting styles and fabrics, think in terms of "packaging". Many of us buy specific brand products at the super markets just because the packages are appealing. The same holds true for clothing-- it's the first impression you leave that makes the difference. Review your physical build and personality as you would your assets and liabilities in borrowing money! Choose garments that will emphasize your assets and camoflauge your liabilities.

Tall figures should avoid vertical lines that add height while shorter persons should choose these lines. Taller persons can wear bold prints and horizontal lines while shorter persons cannot. The woman with a large bust will choose lines that detract from that area--place emphasis at the hips, waist and hem. The pear-shaped person (having hips twelve or more inches larger than the waist) should call attention to the upper part of the body via scarves, necklaces, yokes, collars, and details in the upper dress. Women with broad shoulders will find raglan and dolman sleeves, narrow lapels and vertical lines most flattering.

To help you analyze your figure, Edith Head, leading Hollywood designer, suggests in her book How to Dress for Success slipping a brown paper bag over your head having only holes for your eyes and nose. Wearing a swimsuit or a skin tight fitting undergarment, look at your figure in a mirror very critically. This way, you're not going to be influenced by hair and facial features.

Colors have many roles--so select one according to the job you want done. Dark shades are the most slenderizing. This doesn't necessarily mean you'll be selecting blacks and navies. There are also dark reds, greens, purples and browns.

Pale colors add pounds because they reflect light. Overweight women and those with specific figure problems (heavy hips or thighs) should avoid emphasis in those areas. Possibly a darker shade should be chosen for the skirt or slacks and a pastel for the bodice. Or use pastels for accents.

The warm colors--reds, yellows, oranges--are exciting and gay. They are classified as "advancing colors" -- easily spotted and attracting attention. Again, the overweight person should avoid them because of that reason. But, they can be used by all as accents -- in small quantities.

When you dearly love a color, and it is unbecoming for one reason or another, choose it for underlinings or linings. No one else will know it's there, but you will. It will make sewing and wearing the garment much more fun!!

When matching colors, do so in daylight or under the type of lighting in which they'll be seen when you wear the garment. Lights do change colors!!!

Textures make a difference, too. Shiny and clinging fabrics reveal the figure. They look best on one with perfect proportions. Stiff, crisp fabrics are best for a thin person since they stand away from the figure and fill it out. Heavy, bulky fabrics are too overpowering for the short woman. The tall, thin gal wears them best. Dull-surfaced fabrics are becoming to all. They not only slim the silhouette but also hide figure faults.

It takes time to discover the colors and textures that "do" something for you -- emphasize skin and hair coloring, body build, etc. The fabric department is an excellent place to begin shopping. There you'll find an unlimited assortment of colors, patterns and textures with which to experiment.

Estimating Yardage

Often the pattern envelopes do not include required yardage for all widths of cloth. Use this formula to compute needed amounts when they are not given. Note: When adjusting for a 60" fabric, double check to make certain you are buying the length of the garment.

1. Subtract difference in width between your cloth and one on the envelope having the closest width. (Ex.: Yours= 60"; closest given= 45"; difference= 15".)

2. Multiply difference by number of yards required for closest width. (If 3 yards are required at 45"; multiply 15" by 3; total is 45".)

3. Either add or subtract this amount to the yardage suggested for the closest width given. Add if your width is less; subtract if your cloth is wider. This is the amount to purchase. (3 yards less 45", or 1-3/4 yards should be purchased.)

When selecting plaids, purchase 1/4 to 1/2 yard more for matching smaller plaids, checks or stripes; and 1/2 to one yard more for matching larger plaids or designs.

When buying napped fabrics (velvet, corduroy, velour) additional fabric is needed because all pieces must be cut in the same direction. This is also true for fabrics having a one-way design or pattern.

Preparing Fabric

A common question --
"Do we need to preshrink everything?"

Most fabrics today are finished with 1% maximum shrinkage. When selecting cloth for a garment, check the hangtags or board ends for shrinkage and fiber information. If the tag has been removed, request information from the buyer. If fashion fabric, interfacings and underlinings are labelled 1% maximum shrinkage, then no preshrinking is necessary. All should perform alike, provided everything is cut the same -- all on lengthwise grain, not lengthwise and crosswise combined. If maximum shrinkages vary (fashion fabric with 2% shrinkage and underlining with 1% shrinkage), then one should preshrink all fabrics.

Some fabrics need to be processed to straighten the grain-- this is called "relaxation shrinkage". (Keep in mind, permanent press and fabrics bonded off grain can not be straightened. So, purchase only those that are straight.)

To preshrink washable fabrics, clip selvages and straighten ends of cloth. Then immerse folded cloth in water (the same temperature that would be used for laundering). When thoroughly moistened, remove from water; press out excess moisture. DO NOT WRING. Place loosely woven fabric on a flat surface covered with plastic. If hung over a rod or line, the cloth could stretch. For corduroy, tumble dry to prevent the nap from packing down. For firmly woven cloth, tumble dry or drip-dry.

Process woolens if the hang-tag information does not state "sponged", "ready for needle", or "preshrunk". (Many imported fabrics are not ready for sewing.) Either the "London Shrink" method or steam pressing by a cleaner could be used for processing. Personally, I do not have cloth steam pressed as I have found stretching does occur when the cloth is moved while damp, especially when there is yardage (weight) pulling on both sides of the dampened section.

The London Shrink method also straightens grain. (Do not use on woolens where the cloth would lose some of its finish or where moisture would cause a felting process and the cloth would lose its open-look.) To process woolens in this manner, wet a sheet and wring out excess moisture. Fold fabric in lengthwise direction, basting ends and selvages together. (Clip selvages periodically.) Open sheet, place fabric inside. (a)

a.

b.

Fold sides of sheet over cloth. (b)
Beginning at both ends, fold material every twelve inches. (c)

Cover roll of cloth with a piece of plastic to retain moisture. (d) Leave overnight. (Ample time is required for moisture to penetrate fabric.) Unfold, smooth cloth on a flat surface. DO NOT HANG TO DRY! Additional pressing should not be needed.

c.

(When purchasing fabric, buy the best quality you can afford. It isn't worth your time to underline and spend hours working on a 39¢ cotton or $1.99 woolen.)

d.

Zippers,* bias or seam tape, elastic, and grosgrain ribbon should also be preshrunk because they often shrink more than the fashion fabric. Immerse in a 2-cup measuring cup or bowl of hot water. Remove when water is cool. Hang to drip dry. Rather than removing bias and seam tapes from the cardboard, bend the cardboard. Immerse in water. Remove, and set cardboard on edge so tape drips dry. (Because cardboard is bent, shrinkage is possible. When dry, tape needs no pressing and is already wound on cardboard.)

*With some permanent press fabrics, even a slight shrinking of the zipper tape causes a rippled appearance.

Using Bulky Fabrics

When selecting bulky fabrics (woolens, polyester double knits, etc.) for garments that require facings, eliminate bulk by --

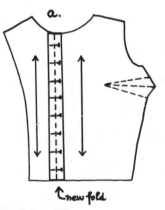

a.

new fold

-- cutting facing on garment. Overlap bodice front and front facing on stitching line (if front edge is on straight of grain). Stitching line will now be the new "fold" line. (a)

-- using lighter weight fabric for facings. If the front seam edge is not on the straight of grain, and if separate facings must be cut, consider using a lighter weight piece of fabric. Lining and underlining fabrics are ideal for dress weight fashion fabrics. For woolen coatings, wool knits and flannel are excellent. These can be used for facings and undercollars.

For professionally finished facings, line them so the outside edges are finished. Cut the facings and linings for each. (Both Siri and SiBonne! are excellent choices for the facing and lining.) Join shoulder seams, then stitch outer edges with right sides together. Trim, turn, stitch facing to garment as usual. See page 68, Fig. e.

Shaping Fabrics

Layer of cloth placed between the fashion fabric and facing, around neck, in collars and cuffs, waistbands and hems. Interfacings give body and extra support for lasting shape and for areas under strain, such as buttons and buttonholes.

Interfacings

Second garment assembled separately and inserted in garments with wrong sides together. Linings protect the shape and seams; cover inside construction; prevent wrinkling; and serve as built-in slips for dresses and skirts.

Linings

Second layer of cloth stitched with fashion fabric. Underlinings stabilize fashion fabric by giving more body, preventing wrinkles, and preventing stretching. They also preserve color, serve as a means for transferring markings from paper patterns to the garment and prevent hemming stitches from showing on the outside. Other terms for underlining include "mounting" or "backing".

Underlinings

Layer of warmth sandwiched between garment and lining, or stitched to either the fashion fabric or lining as an underlining.

Interlinings

How many of us overlook shaping fabrics because they're not seen on the outside??? If one compares sewing to building a sky-scraper, one realizes the importance of inside support. Shaping fabrics not only build but maintain the shape of a garment -- keep it looking "new". These fabrics are extremely important in supplementing and supporting those fashion fabrics that lose some of their body after dry-cleaning and laundering.

Both the silhouette and fashion fabric will help you determine which shaping fabrics to use. An exaggerated silhouette, such as an A-line dress with a stand-up collar, or a fashion fabric with little body will require more inside support than a softer silhouette or fashion fabric with much firmness. Try several shaping fabrics with the fashion fabric. Select the one which feels like the correct amount of support for the style and fashion fabric.

Interfacings

INTERFACINGS should be included in all garments to prevent stretching and give extra reinforcement where needed (under buttons, waistbands, necklines, etc.).

Because there are many weights, types and finishes available, this area seems to be the most confusing for the home-sewer. Generally speaking, unless the garment is cut on the bias or is extremely exaggerated, the interfacing should be the same weight as the fashion fabric -- lightweight with lightweight fabrics. For the bias garment, or stand-up collar, select an interfacing with more firmness. (To determine which weight and firmness is best, slip the interfacing between two pieces of fashion fabric or under the fashion fabric--if used under a yoke. This is how it will be incorporated in the garment so you can check the performance.)

You'll find wovens, non-wovens and hair canvases. Woven fabrics have a lengthwise and crosswise grain. They have strength in both these directions yet give on the bias. Non-wovens are fibers fused together and have no grainline.

The "hair canvas" contains goat hair as one of the fibers. These interfacings are unique from the standpoint that the goat hair prevents creasing. Consequently, they are used in woolens, garments with rolled lapels and collars, garments needing wrinkle resistance and strength, and in softer looking hems. The quality of the hair canvas will determine the price. Those containing some wool will be more expensive than the ones containing cotton and/or rayon in addition to the goat hair. For rolled collars, hair canvases containing wool are easy to steam shape.

Two of the newest fabrics on the market are polyester double knits and permanent press fabrics. For these, a permanent press interfacing should be chosen -- both fabric and interfacing will require little or no ironing.

Iron-on interfacings have a limited use in clothing construction because they are difficult to bond smoothly without pleats and bubbles, and they create a stiff look. You'll recognize them by the sugar-like granules on the wrong side. This is placed on the wrong side of the fashion fabric and pressed with a dry iron, using an up-and-down movement. Iron-on interfacings are most successfully used in small detail areas such as gusset points and bound buttonhole strips. Other uses include fusing to the back of paper pattern pieces to make a "permanent pattern", and bonding to place mats and wall hangings -- items that will not be laundered frequently and need a "stiff look".

TECHNIQUES FOR USING
HAIR CANVASES

Because hair canvases do not crease easily, they must be eliminated from seams. This can be done in three ways:

1) Remove seam allowance and catch-stitch hair canvas next to stitching line;

2) Stitch hair canvas to underlining about 3/4"-1" from edge, and trim hair canvas back to stitching;

3) Stitch bias strip of lightweight cotton or lining about one inch from the edge, and trim back hair canvas to stitching. Then attach interfacing as usual.

STAND-UP COLLARS:

1. Choose heavier interfacing, or sew two pieces together--this is necessary to keep collars "standing".

2. Cut interfacing half the width of the collar. Trim seam allowances; cut diagonally across corners to eliminate bulk. (If interfacing is cut on the bias, arrange so all grainlines are the same direction.)

3. Stitch interfacing to wrong side of undercollar--next to neck-- using either parallel machine or hand padding stitches (from fold to edge of interfacing). (a)

CUTTING FRONT JACKET OR COAT INTERFACING:

When cutting the front interfacing, extend it across the shoulders and around the armhole. If your pattern piece is not cut this way, make a new one.

Draw a line 2" to 2-1/2" below armhole at side seam. Draw another line 1/2" to 1" wider than facing at bottom edge. Connect these with a curved line. (b)

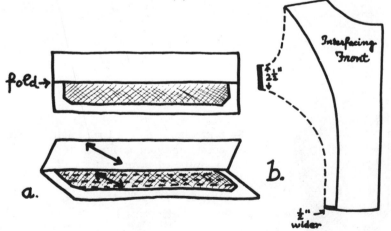

Underlinings - Linings

UNDERLININGS AND LININGS are often confused -- they're both "shape retainers". And, underlinings are "shape-builders". Both can be the same fabric, yet are incorporated in the garment in two different ways. When stitched in the seams with the fashion fabric, it's called an "underlining". When assembled separately, as a second garment and hung inside the garment, then it's called a "lining". You'll find linings, underlinings, or a combination of both in better ready-to-wear garments. Manufacturers KNOW their importance in giving shape to garments and keeping the shape. From ready-to-wear garments we learn that those professional looking garments usually have either a lining or underlining, or both.

To further explain "keeping the shape", remember that wrinkling and "rump spring" or "seating" are both caused by a combination of three factors--moisture, heat and pressure. In other words, your body works like a steam iron--producing perspiration (moisture), maintaining a 98.6° temperature, and adding pressure when you are sitting. If one or two of these factors can be removed, the outer fashion fabric will not sag, stretch or wrinkle. This is where under-linings and linings are vital--they absorb perspiration and take the strain from the fashion fabric (because they are firmly woven fabrics).

Because underlinings are stitched in the seams, they also lend extra support for exaggerated silhouettes or too-soft fabrics. They preserve color for loosely woven fabrics and sheers. And, they are used for anchoring a hem without stitches showing on the outside of the garment.

I personally underline all my garments, including bondeds and light-weight knits. If I want a built-in slip, seam protection and the construction covered, I also add a lining. Yes, I do either line or underline bonded fabrics and knits. With both these cloths, "rump spring" is a common problem. Keep in mind that bonded fabrics are usually loosely woven or knit materials attached to a knit tricot backing. Both outer fabric and backing will "give". True, bonded fabrics are easier to cut and sew because they have more firmness than a loosely woven cloth; however, to prevent stretching, either an underlining or lining is necessary.

If you check the better quality ready-to-wear double knits that are not lined, you'll notice many are two-to three-times the weight of knits available in fabric departments. This is why they are not lined--they stretch and return to their original shape. Remember the problem home-sewers had with jersey--before it was bonded and before double knits were available? Again, because it was so light in weight, it stretched and sagged. (For the light-weight double knits, ranging from $3-$7 a yard, I underline if the silhouette is exaggerated and my fabric needs more support. Or, if it's a softer looking style, then I line. I usually just line or underline the body section only and retain the stretchy property of the knit in the sleeves for additional movement).

which one has the Underlining?

The Underlined Dress

When underlining a garment, you are actually creating a new piece of fashion fabric with a new personality--with added body and stability. Yet, in order for the underlining to do its job, it is imperative that underlinings be correct in size and smooth on the inside of the garment.

Many women are complaining because the underlining (when stitched flat to the flat fashion fabric) buckles and is too big inside the garment causing pleats and creases in both the horizontal and vertical directions. When this happens, the underlining can not perform its job--and even though you've underlined the garment, it will still sag and stretch. With sheer and light-weight fabrics, these creases also show on the outside of the garment. As you know, when using an embroidery hoop, the inside ring must be smaller in order to fit. The same is true for the underlining. In order for it to fit smoothly on the body and do its job, the inner piece of cloth must be a little smaller than the outside garment. Rather than cutting the underlining smaller, it's safer to use this "pinning and folding" method. We will remove any excess underlining in the crosswise direction in parts of the garment that encircle the body--skirt, dress below armholes, slacks, sleeves, jacket body under armholes. Before we hem the garment, we'll also eliminate any excess under-lining in the lengthwise direction. Otherwise, the hem attached to underlining only may begin sagging at center front or back.

1. Cut underlining first, then fashion fabric from the same pattern piece. Cut separately for accuracy--with bulky fabrics the paper pattern sometimes rips while being cut. (Cut underlining on the straight of grain. If the garment is cut on the bias, the underlining can either be cut on the straight of grain or bias depending on effect desired. For an exaggerated shape or for loosely woven fashion fabric, cut the underlining on the straight of

grain. For a soft look, cut underlining
on the bias.)

2. Cut interfacing. Cut diagonally
at corners to eliminate bulk. (a)

3. A shortcut--stitch interfacing
for neck to underlining (5/8"
from edge) before underlining is
joined to fashion fabric. Trim
interfacing back to stitching. (b)

4. When joining underlining to wrong
side of fashion fabric, keep interfacings and markings up--away
from fashion fabric. (Darts,
tucks and dots are transferred
from pattern to underlining only.)

5. For a one-piece back or front,
pin-baste underlining to fashion
fabric at center front or center
back with pins parallel to lengthwise grain at center. (c)

6. Fold the garment from center
toward one side. Smooth underlining toward edge so
excess slips into side
seam allowance. Pin
along edge from top
to bottom with pins
parallel. Do same
for opposite side.

7. For the two-part front or
   back and sleeves, pin-baste
   underlining to fashion fabric
   along one side with pins
   parallel to edge. Fold the
   garment from the pinned side
   toward the other side. Smooth
   underlining toward edge so
   excess slips into seam
   allowance. (d)

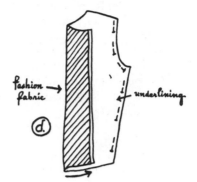

   (There should be <u>no more
   than 3/8"-1/2" total slippage</u>
   for the front half; the same
   for back half, sleeves, slacks.
   And, there should be <u>little or
   no slippage</u> across the chest
   where the garment fits flat
   against the body. The amount
   of slippage depends on the
   fashion fabric and underlining.
   You'll find more with silk and
   a silky underlining than a
   textured woolen and a cottony
   underlining. For those silky
   fabrics, control the total
   slippage!) (e)

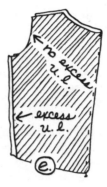

8. Trim excess underlining from
   seam allowance so edges of
   fashion fabric and underlining
   are together. (f)

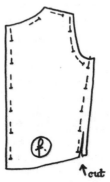

9. If garment to be underlined has a dart, then baste fashion fabric
and underlining together through center of dart before staystitching outer edges of garment together. <u>Baste through center
of dart from point to wide end</u>, beginning a few stitches beyond
the point. (By basting through center of the dart from the point,
any excess underlining will slip into
the outside seam allowance. Otherwise, you may have a "bubble" at
the point.)

--When stitching the dart, sew
as you normally would--,
from the wide end to the
point. (g)

10. To staystitch underlining to
fashion fabric:

--Stitch with underlining up
always. Fashion fabric should be
next to the feed dog of the sewing
machine. (Do not stitch one side
with underlining up and other side
with fashion fabric up. These fabrics
feed into the machine at different rates.
Consequently, you'll be creating diagonal
wrinkles in the outer fabric
when this is done.)

--Use 10 stitches per inch at 1/2"
from edge except at neck edge--
then stitch at almost 5/8" from
edge. This provides reinforcement for clipping that curved edge
when collars or facings are
attached. If your machine pressure
is too heavy, you'll find a bubble
at the corners when you pivot. Either adjust, or DO NOT PIVOT
at corners. Instead, stitch to seamlines and stop; or stitch
off material. (h)

--Stitch in the same direction on both sides of the garment piece, even though it may be more bulky to do so. (i) For stitching the left side, one must roll bulk of fabric and place under the arm of the machine. (j) For a seam guide, use masking or adhesive tape or cellophane tape over a colored string on the throat plate area of the machine. (By stitching from top to bottom, even though it is against the grain, any excess underlining will slip into the hem rather than buckling at the top of the hem. There is also no stretching of any consequence because underlinings are firmly woven. If you stitch from hem to waist and top to waist, you'll have buckling at the waistline!)

start

i.

11. Before hemming garment, smooth excess underlining into the hem before the hem is turned up. Trim any excess from hem edge. Pin fashion fabric and underlining edges together, with underlining up. (Ease fashion fabric in position.) Stitch with underlining up.

j.

Lining a dress or skirt

1. Cut lining from same pattern pieces, except for facings, as garment. Make one inch shorter in length (skirt or shift).

2. Construct lining separately.

3. Insert in dress or skirt after side, back and shoulder seams have been stitched and zipper has been installed. Place wrong sides together.

4. Baste around neck and armholes in dress and waist in skirt. Turn under seam allowance where zipper is installed. Pin to zipper tape in dress and stitch by hand using two rows of stitching-- a slip stitch to anchor in place, and a running stitch about 1/4" away to prevent lining from rolling into zipper teeth and getting caught. In skirt, it is not necessary to attach to zipper tape.

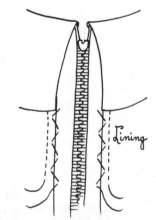

5. Stitch on facings at neck and armholes or set-in sleeves in dress. In skirt, attach waistband.

Sleeveless Vests

...lining to edge...

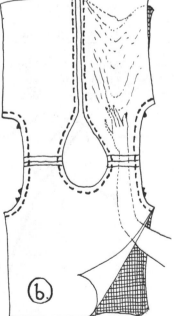

1. Cut lining from same pattern as fashion fabric for garment. Do not allow pleat at center back. Cut 1/4" less in width at shoulders, tapering to nothing at notches. (a)

2. Stitch shoulder seams only on lining and shoulder seams only on garment. (Underlinings, interfacings, pockets, flaps--all should be attached. DO NOT MAKE BUTTONHOLES YET, UNLESS BOUND.)

3. Pin lining to vest with right sides together. Stitch at 5/8" around armholes, neck and front. DO NOT SEW SIDE SEAMS TOGETHER.

4. Trim seam allowances; clip curved edges.

5. Pull front sections through shoulder opening--between fashion fabric and lining. (b)

6. Press. Understitch.

7. Sew side seams--place right sides of fashion fabric together and right sides of lining. Make one continuous seam. Press open. Turn lining down over garment, so wrong sides are together.

8. Hem garment and lining by hand.

9. Topstitch. Sew buttonholes and buttons.

Jacket or Coat Linings

PURPOSE: to cover inside construction.
Therefore, they should be a
little larger than outside
garment to prevent binding
and fit smoothly.

CUTTING: These linings should include an <u>open shoulder dart</u>, <u>one</u>
<u>inch pleat</u> down center back and a pleat at edge of hem.

1. The commercial pattern usually has a separate pattern piece
for the lining front and back. The sleeve pattern of the jacket
is used. Make the same alterations on these patterns that
were made for the jacket or coat.

2. <u>IF PATTERN HAS NO LINING PATTERN PIECES, THEN --</u>

Mark the width of the front and neck facings on bodice pattern
(1-a). Measure 1-1/4" toward front and neck edges (from edge
of facings). Mark. This is new cutting line (1-b).

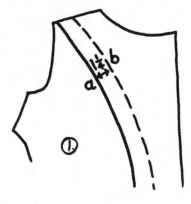

In length, the back and front
are cut to the unhemmed length
less one inch. The sleeves,
the unhemmed length less 3/4".
(These measurements are
for garments having a 1 1/2"
minimum hem or wider.)

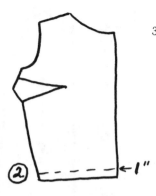

3. <u>MAKING PLEAT AT BOTTOM:</u>
Cut lining same length as garment
before hemming, less one inch.
(2)

--After hem of jacket or coat is
stitched in position, stitch bottom
edge of lining to top edge of hem
by hand. This also prevents the
inside construction from being
seen.

4. <u>MAKING SHOULDER DART:</u> Slash through center of
shoulder seam toward bust point. (3)

Close underarm and/or waist darts. This automatically
throws open the new slashed area. Insert tissue under
slash. Tape. (4-a) To obtain correct outer edge of
dart, fold so slashed edges are together with bulk of
paper toward neck edge. Cut across shoulder cutting
line. (4-b) Draw dart following slashed edge, stopping
one inch from bust point.

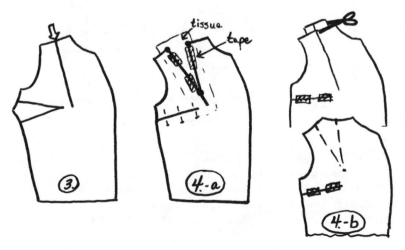

--To stitch open dart, bring slashed edges together. Stitch
down about 1-1/2". Press toward neck edge. (This forms
open dart.)

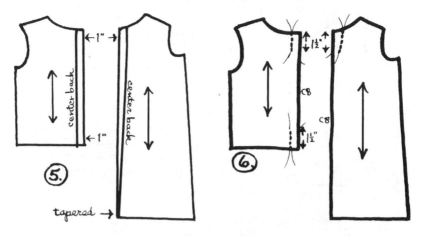

5. **MAKING CENTER BACK PLEAT:** For jacket, add one inch
    at top and bottom along center back. For coat, add one inch
    at top and taper to nothing at bottom. (5)

    --To stitch: Machine stitch at center back about 1-1/2" down
    from top and above bottom for jacket; then press pleat toward
    right back. Stitch at center back about 1-1/2" from top for
    coat. Press pleat toward right back. (6)

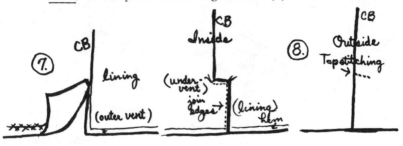

6. **LINING JACKET WITH PLEAT OR VENT:**
    Stitch CB seam of lining above pleat or vent.
    Turn under edge of lining for outer vent.
    Slipstitch to vent. (7) Place lining for under **vent**
    on edge; machine or hand stitch together. Top-
    stitch through all thicknesses at top of pleat or
    vent. (8)

Lining by Machine

1. Cut pieces as discussed under "cutting" - number 1 to 5, pages 26-28.

2. Press jacket or coat thoroughly.

3. Staystitch neck and front edges of lining on seamlines. Clip curved edges. Sew gathering thread at seamline of sleeve cap.

4. Stitch darts and center back pleats. Sew side seams and shoulder seams of body lining. Press. Stitch seams of sleeve lining.

5. Sew sleeves to body lining unit. Press. Trim seam allowance at underarm seam area -- same way garment armhole was finished.

6. Pin neck and front edges of lining to facings. Stitch at 5/8" from center back to bottom edge. Press seams toward lining. (Clip where necessary.)

7. Position sleeve lining within sleeves--using stab stitch to anchor sleeve seam allowances together. Turn under bottom hem of lining -- pin to sleeve hem. Use slip stitch to fasten together at hem edge.

8. Use stab stitch * to fasten shoulder edge of armholes and underarm edges of armholes. (*See page 44 for stitch)

Lining by Hand

(The bodice part is assembled and inserted by hand; and the sleeve is assembled and inserted last by hand.)

1. The jacket or coat must be carefully and thoroughly pressed before attaching the lining. Once the lining is in, it will hinder pressing.

2. When cutting the lining, add to the following areas to make certain lining is slightly larger and will not bind inside garment.

   -- 1/2" at armhole edge of underarm seam, tapering to nothing at waist.
   -- 1-1/2" to shoulder seam width on both lining front and back, tapering to nothing at armhole notches.
   -- 1" to length of underarm seam (at armhole) of sleeve lining.

3. Staystitch only back neck edge on seamline. Sew gathering thread at seamline of sleeve cap between notches.

4. Sew side seams of jacket and sleeve seams by machine. DO NOT STITCH SHOULDER SEAMS. Stitch shoulder darts and center back pleats. (See numbers 3 and 5 under "cutting", pages 27-28.) Press.

inside
Underlining   Facing

Lining

ⓐ.

5. Pin bottom edge of lining to hem of jacket. Stitch 1/4" from edge using small running stitches. (a)

6. Bring lining up to shoulder, smoothing around armhole in front. Pin. Then smooth around back armhole. Turn under back shoulder seam allowance. Overlap on front seam allowance. Pin. (b)

7. Slash back neck to stitching. Turn under seam allowance and pin to neck and front facings.

8. Fell stitch lining edge to facings. Hand baste lining to armhole for about 2 inches at shoulder seam and underarm seams. Trim any excess lining. (c)

9. Turn sleeves of garment inside out. Sew underarm seams of sleeve linings.

10. With right side of lining hem edge on right side of sleeve hem, stitch together 1/4" from edge using small running stitches. (Same as jacket hem edges. --a)

11. Turn sleeve right side out. Pull lining up inside sleeves. Tack underarm seamline of sleeve lining to sleeve using stab stitch.

12. Pin-baste sleeve lining over bodice lining at armhole. Turn under more than 5/8" seam allowance at cap of sleeve (lining) if there is extra fullness. Fell sleeve lining by hand to bodice lining, catching seam allowances of outer garment only at shoulder and underarm seams. (Clip sleeve seam allowance where needed.)

Interlinings

--not the same as "underlining." It adds extra warmth and is used in coats.

1. To apply, either sandwich a loosely woven woolen (ARMO-WOOL), or outing flannel between lining and outer garment, or underline lining or fashion fabric.

2. Some materials have built-in warmth, such as:

   --Sunbak: a satin face with napped back.
   --Quilted nylon or acetate satin.

DESIGNER TOUCHES WITH LAMBSWOOL:

PADDING SLEEVE CAPS:

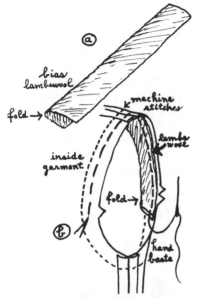

To maintain a smooth sleevecap in
coats and suits, hand-baste bias
cut lambswool in the cap area after
the sleeve has been permanently
stitched in the garment (but before
the lining is inserted).

Cut a bias piece of woven lambswool,
2 inches wide and 8 inches long. Fold
in half in the lengthwise direction. (a)
Hand-baste in cap, centering piece
at shoulder seam, so cut edges of
bias are on cut edges of armhole
seam. (b)

Lambswool will fill the void area
between the seam and sleeve cap.
Without it, small wrinkles exist.

SOFT PLEATS AT CENTER FRONT OF SKIRTS/DRESSES:

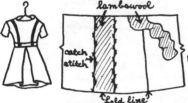

To maintain a soft, un-pressed look
with a center front pleat, catchstitch a bias strip of lambswool to
the underlining over the fold line.
Cut bias strip about 2 1/2"-3" wide.

SOFT EDGES OF GARMENTS:

Cut several layers of lambswool
as wide as the desired padded edge,
following pattern piece. (For hem
border, cut the shape of the skirt.
For collars, follow grainline and
shape of collar.) Insert in collar,
belt, or inside hem or neckline.
Hand-baste to hold in place; then
topstitch, making rows of stitches
at least 1/2" apart.

Tips with Tricots

For many years it was difficult to construct tricot and spandex garments at home. Today, with these fabrics readily available, the advent of synthetic threads and new stitches on sewing machines, anyone can create daywear, loungewear and nightwear garments.

In working with knit tricots, remember that they do not have a straight grainline like woven fabrics. Instead, you'll find ribs in the lengthwise direction (right side of fabric) and ribs in the crosswise direction (wrong side of fabric). For pattern layout, use the vertical ribs as a guide (as you did lengthwise grain in woven fabrics).

Since maximum stretch is in the crosswise direction, cut garments so maximum stretch goes around the body! (a)

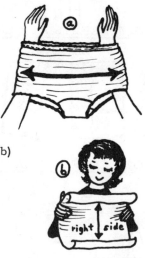

To determine the right side of the tricot, stretch the cut edge in the crosswise direction. The cut edge will curl toward the right (b) side of the cloth. (In constructing a gown having a handkerchief hem, take advantage of this curling by constructing the garment with the wrong side of the knit out. Use the floating stitch for hemming--#1 on page 42.)

To duplicate a favorite ready-to-wear girdle, bra or pair of panties, use aluminum foil for making a pattern. You'll be able to locate seams, panels and curves in the correct locations for you. For more details, see page 143.

PINS AND NEEDLES:

Special ball-point needles and pins
are highly recommended where spandex
fabrics are used. Because these yarns
are heavier, puncturing them would cause
loss of strength and stretch. Use these
pins and needles with girdle, swimwear
and skiwear fabrics,and in attaching elastic.
For tricot fabrics, use a sharp
#9 or #11 needle and sharp, dressmaker
pins.

STITCHING:

Use about 12 stitches per inch; balanced tension; double
rows of straight stitching (1/4" apart) or a combination of
straight stitching and zigzagging at the seam edge. (c) With
threads that "give", no seams will pop! Check presser
foot pressure by stitching on two thicknesses of fabric before
sewing on actual garment. Pin two 8" strips of fabric at
both ends. Machine stitch without removing pins. If
pressure is correct, both pieces of fabric will be together
at the ends without buckling. If buckling occurs, then adjust.

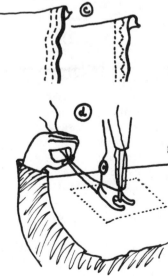

Backstitching causes jamming in
the throatplate opening. As you begin
to stitch seams,hold both upper and
lower threads to the rear of the
machine. (d)
Clean needle frequently. Due to
static electricity, lint builds up in eye
so that it could interfere with tension.
To prevent puckered looking seams,
gently stretch fabric as you stitch.
Skipped stitches may mean a
slightly bent needle or the need for a
ball point needle.   DO NOT STITCH OVER
PINS--remove as you stitch.

STITCHING ELASTIC:

Choose from tunnel elastic, lingerie elastic or elastic lace. Cut elastic 2"-8" shorter than your measurements, depending on type elastic chosen. Check length for personal comfort.

For lingerie elastic and elastic lace, seam ends to make circle before attaching to garment. Seam with right sides together (a). Open seam; stitch a rectangle to secure ends (b). Divide elastic circle in 8 parts using pins. Divide garment opening in 8 parts, also. Position elastic so seam is at side seam of garment. Match pins (c).

For flat application, place wrong side of elastic to right side of garment. Stitch lower edge of elastic to garment, stretching as you stitch. Stitch upper edge of elastic. Trim excess tricot close to stitching(d).

For stitched and turned application, place elastic circle on garment so wrong sides are together. Stitch lower edge of elastic, stretching as you sew. Trim tricot close to stitching (e). Turn elastic to right side of garment. Stitch lower edge to garment, stretching as you stitch (f).

For tunnel elastic, fold tricot to wrong side and make casing the width of the elastic plus 1/8". Leave a small opening so tunnel elastic can be inserted. Join ends of elastic by hand. Finish stitching opening by hand. For a quick casing--Stitch elastic in circle. On wrong side of garment, fold tricot to cover elastic circle and stitch 4"-5". Continue folding and stitching until elastic circle is covered. Be careful not to catch elastic when stitching.

ATTACHING LACE:

To hold in position while stitching, use either sharp pins or transparent mending tape. If lace is to be stitched to edge of garment, place 1/2"-3/4" above edge of fabric. After stitching, trim excess tricot.

With beading lace, merely stitch lace over satin ribbon rather than threading ribbon through lace.

Miter lace corner by sewing off lace and fabric on one side (g). Pivot lace to other side of corner until lace is smooth against garment. Stitch through folded lace near fold, then trim excess lace from wrong side (h). Stitch second side in place.

STRAPS FOR GOWNS OR SLIPS:

Cut approximately 2" longer than needed. Place edge of strap on edge of garment with right sides together. Stitch at the end and 1" below edge (i). Turn strap up in position. Stitch again at edge (j).

Select from self-color satin straps, or use one of these alternatives:
1- Elastic lace; 2- Narrow satin ribbon under beading lace; 3- Lace on double tricot (stitched and turned); 4- Satin ribbon under lace, leaving extension of ribbon at end for a loop (k); 5- Double sheer tricot , 2" wide after stitched and turned, gathered where attached to gown (l); 6- Double sheer tricot with narrow bindings at each edge; 7- One, two or three spaghetti straps of sheer or opaque tricot; 8- Two spaghetti straps looped at center. Make two straps for each side of garment. Stitch both ends of one strap to front of gown forming a loop. Insert second strap through loop and stitch to back of gown (m).

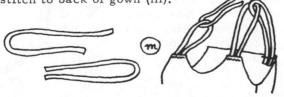

BINDINGS:

Cut tricot in crosswise direction six times the desired width. Pin in half in the lengthwise direction. Place doubled strip with raw edges matching raw edges of garment on right side of garment. Follow instructions for "Hong Kong Finish", page 92. Since stitching is done by machine, binding is securely attached. Stitching doesn't show since it was done in the crevice where the binding was attached to the garment.

OTHER POINTERS:

Eliminate seam at front edge of sheer peignoirs by overlapping front and facing pattern pieces at stitching lines. Cut as one piece. Or, cut front pieces double with fold at front edge.

To turn narrow spaghetti straps, cut a small hole in the fold about an inch from the end. Secure a safety pin from end through hole. Work pin through tubing until reversed (n). For a rounded look, leave seam allowance ; for flat look, trim seam allowance.

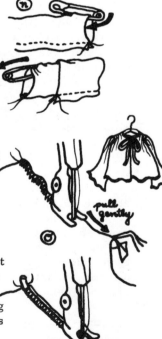

For a fluted bottom edge on gowns and sleeves, use a satin stitch and pull tricot gently as you stitch (o). Also, a heavier piece of thread or cording can be placed on fabric edge and covered by satin stitch (p).

For tricot blouses with button closures, interface facing with bias-cut permanent press fabric. Zigzag edges of interfacing and tricot together to prevent tricot from curling. Cut facing and front as one (overlap stitching lines at front edge) to eliminate a seam and possible curling at the front edge.

Create exciting color combinations in peignoirs, gowns and panties by using two different colors for the opaque tricot and sheer tricot overlay. Experiment with darks (sheers) over lights or lights over darks!

To install zipper in tricot garments, select the lightweight nylon or polyester coil zippers. Cut a bias strip of permanent press interfacing about one inch wide and stitch to seamline where zipper will be installed. This gives soft support and will prevent stretching of the seam. See page 204.

For hems of dresses or tunics made from tricot, give extra firmness and prevent curling by enclosing a bias strip of interfacing in the hem. Cut the same with as the hem. Stitch near edge of hem and fold by machine before hem is stitched in position by hand. See page 88.

To change a regular sleeve to a full sleeve, see page 59.

For closures on sheer dusters and peignoirs, use a ribbon or tricot tie, snaps or loops.

In addition to buying beautiful lace appliques, many wide laces have floral patterns that could be cut out and used as appliques. (To attach, tape in position and stitch following outline of applique.)

Anti-static tricot is not only excellent for skirt savers but can be used for uniforms and tennis dresses. Opaque tricot is an excellent underlining for two-way stretch type fabrics (panne velvet, stretch terry, etc.) where   some stretch control is needed. Also, use satin finished tricots for lining knit jackets and coats and as fitted bed or crib sheets and pillow cases.

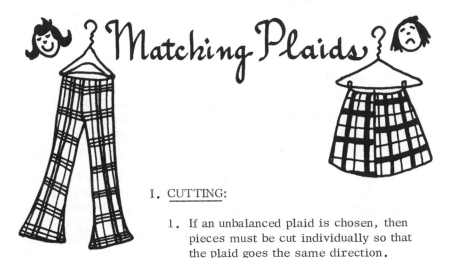

I. <u>CUTTING</u>:

 1. If an unbalanced plaid is chosen, then pieces must be cut individually so that the plaid goes the same direction.

2. If an A-line skirt is to be cut on the bias, do not cut with center front and center back on the fold. Instead, make a pattern for the entire front and back. This will make matching easier.

3. Use corresponding notches for matching--ex.: notch 7 on the front and back pattern pieces should be in the same position of the plaid.

4. If you cannot match both side seams and shoulder seams, then plan to match side seams--a mis-match is much more obvious here.

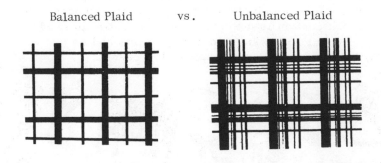

Balanced Plaid   vs.   Unbalanced Plaid

II. SEWING:

--for a definite match without slippage during stitching, try "slip basting." True, it's more time-consuming, but essential in matching plaids and stripes.

1. Working from the right side of the garment, turn under and press seam allowance on one of garment parts. Overlap this seam allowance on joining part. Pin in position.

2. From the right side of the garment, make a short perpendicular stitch--catching a couple yarns in the fold and in the fabric underneath. (a) Use single strand (contrasting color) thread.

3. Slip needle through fold of upper piece and repeat.

4. Turn garment to wrong side. Stitch permanently (by machine) close to the basting stitch in the fold. (b)

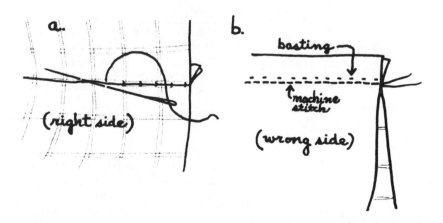

Hand Stitches

1. FLOATING OR SLIP
   STITCH for inside hemming.
   On garment side catch one yarn
   in fold, then take a stitch
   through edge of hem. For
   invisible hem, do not pull
   stitches tight. (For knits, use
   this stitch. Before making a
   knot at the end, leave 5"
   thread. Then put hands inside
   dress and stretch hem so
   stitches are loose. Tie knot
   and cut excess thread. This
   eliminates the problem of
   stitches breaking while walking.)

2. CATCH STITCH for inside
   hemming: a somewhat elastic
   stitch used with knits, also.
   Working from left to right,
   needle pointing from right to
   left, take a stitch through edge
   of hem. Then on garment side
   take a stitch in fold.

3. CATCH STITCH for flat
   surface: because of its elasticity,
   this stitch is used for attaching
   interfacing to the front edge of
   knit garments, flat hems, bias
   collars, etc. Again work from
   left to right, needle pointing
   from right to left. Take a
   stitch next to edge of hem;
   then take a stitch in hem.
   Make stitches loose and even.

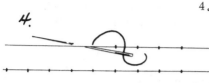

4. BLIND HEMMING OR FELL STITCH: used extensively for taping interfacing in tailoring. Work from right to left taking short perpendicular stitches through tape and fabric, then passing needle through interfacing. Small stitches hold tape firmly.

5. BACK STITCH: strongest of hand stitches. It is used for hand picking (top stitching) and hand sewn zippers. For zippers, stitches are about 1/16" in length and spaced about 3/16" apart.

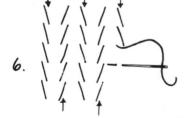

6. PADDING STITCH: a miniature version of tailor basting used to permanently join interfacing to underside of fabric such as under-collar. It is used with lapels, cuffs, collars or any section having a permanent roll or where firmness and some stiffness is required. This diagonal stitch picks up one yarn from underside of outer fabric or underlining. Stitches should be with the grain of the fabric or parallel to a break - or creaseline. Make stitches 1/4" to 1/2" in length, and 1/2" to 3/8" apart. Stitching thread should not be pulled tight. While stitching, hold over forefinger when padding. Steam to shape before and after padding stitch is done.

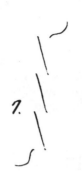

7. TAILOR BASTING: used to
    join two layers of fabric, such
    as underlining to fashion fabric,
    interfacing to underlining, or
    interfacing to fashion fabric.
    If work is done from outside of
    garment, then stitching is
    classified as temporary and
    must be removed. If stitching
    is done from the inside, it can
    either be temporary or per-
    manent. Use long diagonal
    basting on upper side and short
    horizontal stitches on underside.
    Diagonal stitches could be 1" to
    2-1/2" in length, depending upon
    garment.

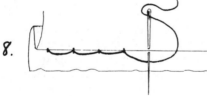

8. BLANKET STITCH OR HALF-
    FEATHER STITCH: a locked
    stitch, permitting greater
    distance between stitches. Work
    from left to right. Not only is
    this stitch used for hems but
    also to attach the free edge of
    interfacings to underlinings or
    fashion fabrics. For coats,
    stitches are usually 2" apart and
    loose; for jackets and dresses,
    1" to 1-1/2" apart.

CROSS VIEW - STAB STITCH

upper collar

under collar

9. STAB STITCH: a running stitch
    used to fasten two seamlines
    together (such as upper and
    under collars). Stitch in seam-
    line, making stitches about 1/16"
    in length. At an angle, push
    needle through all thickness.
    Catch 2-3 yarns of fabric, then
    force needle back through at
    angle again.

Top Stitching

Topstitching is generally considered a decorative stitch, yet is functional in keeping seams flat especially with today's fashion fabrics--polyester knits, permanent press fabrics, vinyls, leathers and suedes.

1. Use long stitches--6-8 per inch.

2. Thread: Use silk buttonhole twist as the top thread with either a size 14 or 16 needle. (With some machines, buttonhole twist will not thread through the upper part of the machine. If this is so, use it in the bobbin, and stitch from the wrong side.) Or, try double strand thread in the top of the machine, using two spools of thread. For cottons and rayons, use mercerized cotton; for permanent press and polyester knits, use polyester thread; for woolens and silks, use silk thread. (When you can't find a good color match with silk buttonhole twist, again use double strand thread instead.)

3. To prevent stitches from sinking into softer fabrics, cut bias (a) strips of hair canvas and place under area to be stitched. For added depth with satins, crepes, and leather, use a strip of lambswool under the area to be topstitched.

4. To keep stitches even, place masking or cellophane tape along stitching lines and follow edge of tape. (b)   It's great on all fabrics except those with nap. For napped or loosely woven fabrics, use the quilting guide (attachment that comes with sewing machine) and zipper foot.

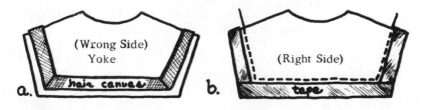

a. (Wrong Side) Yoke   hair canvas

b. (Right Side)   tape

5. Topstitching front edge: If button, when in position, is on top of stitching, (c) add extra width to front edge of bodice and facing patterns before cutting fabric. (d)

6. Hand-picking: Stitching by hand is often best to use especially when fabric is textured. Make backstitch* about 1/16" in length and stitches about 1/4" apart. For even gauging of stitches, pin strip of 1/4" graph paper or notebook paper next to area. (e)

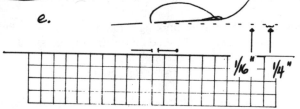

--To prevent tangling of thread when hand-stitching:

   a. Wax strands with beeswax.
   b. Tie each strand separately when using double strand thread.
   c. Thread needle as thread comes from spool. Tie knot at end where thread is cut from spool.

(*Use buttonhole twist, three strands embroidery thread, or double strand mercerized cotton.)

Gathering

1. For softer looking gathers, gathers should hang with the lengthwise grain. Cut skirt, etc. with lengthwise grain perpendicular
   to floor.

2. Use two rows of gathering stitches--one at 1/2" and the other
   at 3/4" from the edge. Gathers will be perpendicular to edge
   because permanent stitching will be done at 5/8" -- in between
   the two rows of gathering. The 3/4" row of stitching is
   temporary and will be removed.

3. In joining a gathered section to another, stitch with the
   gathered part up -- away from feed dog of machine.

4. To prevent the thread from breaking while gathering, use
   either silk or nylon thread in the bobbin, and PULL BOBBIN
   THREAD!

5. For eased skirts with heavier fabrics, make several darts in
   front and back, then ease remainder of cloth. This gives a
   more flattering appearance -- doesn't add inches to the waist
   and hip areas.

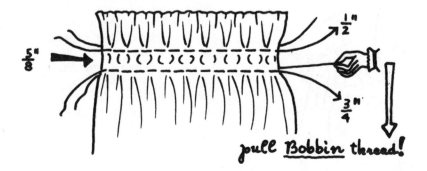

pull Bobbin thread!

Understitching

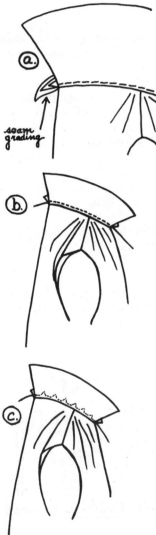

(a.)

seam grading

(b.)

(c.)

(also called "control stitching")

1. Understitching gives a sharp
   edge where facings are
   stitched. It keeps facings
   turned to the wrong side and
   prevents them from showing
   at the neckline and armholes.

2. Where interfacings and
   facings have been applied,
   grade seams (a) so none are
   the same width. The widest
   seam allowance should be
   the part of the garment
   receiving the most strain.
   (At the neck, the bodice seam
   allowance would be the longest.)

3. Press seams toward facings.
   From the wrong side of facing,
   stitch seam allowance to
   facing with stitches parallel
   to seam. Use either regular
   machine stitches (b) or the
   invisible machine hemming
   stitch (c). (The hemming
   stitch is helpful in keeping
   curved, clipped areas flat.)

Darts

I. <u>MARKING</u>:

    1. When garment is underlined, save time by marking darts on underlining with tracing wheel and paper.

2. Use tailor tacks for sheers or when other types of markings would show.

3. When cutting fabric, snip into seam allowance to mark wide end of darts. Use pins to mark points.

4. Use tailor's chalk for leather, suede and fabrics where needle holes or tracing wheel markings would show.

II. <u>STITCHING</u>:

    1. Catch only a few threads at the point, tapering to nothing. An abrupt point will create a "dimple."

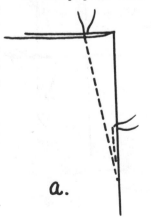

    2. To backstitch at point of dart: sew to point catching only a few threads, then lift presser foot and needle. Insert needle in cloth about 1/4" back from point. Backstitch in dart area. (a)

a.

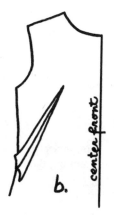

b.   center front

3. Prevent rippling of French darts by slashing down center toward point before stitching. Stitch as a seam. (b)

4. On sheer fabrics, avoid the knot from showing at the tip of the dart by "bobbin stitching." Using bobbin thread, thread machine backward. Pull thread about three times the length of the dart. Sew dart from point to wide end. The first stitch at the point of the dart will have no loose threads. Rethread for each dart.

5. Stagger darts when fabric is bulky:

--Split and trim excess from wide end. Press open. (c)

--Trim upper layer and under layer so neither is the same width. (d)

6. For double-ended darts (found in more fitted shifts), begin stitching at center of dart. Stitch toward each point. Clip at waistline, press toward center front or center back. (e) If stitched from top to bottom, bubbles are often created at the upper point.

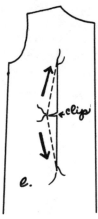

e.   clip

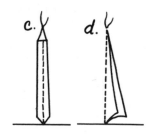

c.   d.

III. <u>PRINCESS LINES:</u>

--In place of darts, they are
incorporated in the seam line.
The seams usually are from center
of shoulder over bustline to waist,
or from underarm over bustline to
waist.

1. Staystitch curved part on seamline.
   Clip to stitching.

2. In joining curved section to center
   front or center back panel, stitch with
   curved part up. Because the seam
   allowance has been clipped, it will be
   flat and easy to stitch.

3. If one section is cut on the bias and other section on
   straight of grain, place bias section next to feed dog of
   machine when seaming. It will ease naturally during
   stitching and sew in evenly.

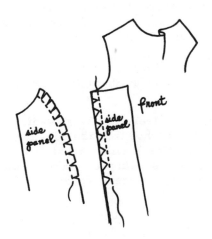

Sleeves

ADJUSTING UPPER ARM CIRCUMFERENCE:

A common problem! In this area (where sleeve joins arm-hole), the pattern should equal your measurement plus 2-1/2" ease for dresses or blouses, 4-1/2" ease for suits, and 5-1/2" ease for coats. Use measurement from larger arm if both are not the same. (a)

1. To adjust sleeve, slash pattern from bottom to top and toward side seams. (b)

2. Spread pattern the needed amount, adding nothing in width at the top or bottom edges. (As you spread, you'll notice a horizontal overlap where slashes were made toward the sides. This is necessary to keep pattern flat and enable you to add only in the upper arm area.) (c)

3. For a short sleeve, add the same amount at both the upper arm area and bottom edge of the sleeve.

4. Measure sleeve cap height--distance from where sleeve is stitched into armhole and edge of shoulder seam. Check same on pattern. Add to top of pattern if needed, tapering to nothing at the notches. (d) (Check ease at cap of sleeve--page 54.)

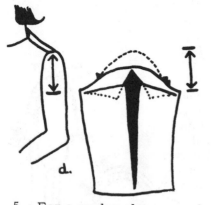

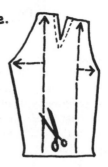

5. For a raglan sleeve, make two slashes--one on each side of the shoulder dart or seam. Slash from bottom to top and over toward side seams where sleeve is set into armhole. (e)

6. Spread pattern the needed amount, adding nothing at the top or bottom (unless it is a short sleeve) edges. (f)

CORRECT POSITIONING OF SLEEVES:

In order for a sleeve to hang freely without wrinkles when worn, the lengthwise grain is perpendicular to the floor and crosswise grain is **parallel** to the floor.(h) If the crosswise grain tilts forward, dial sleeve back. (g) If the crosswise grain tilts backward, dial sleeve forward. (i)

Baste sleeves into armholes matching notches. Check grainline before stitching permanently.

On the first garment, underarm seams of the sleeve and garment may not match, nor will notches and dots. Once you've determined how much a sleeve must be dialed, on future garments the underarm sleeve seam can be shifted as well as the notches and shoulder dot.

CHECK AMOUNT OF EASE AT SLEEVE CAP:

Of all the types of sleeves found in clothing construction, the set-in sleeve presents the most problems. Because the sleeve cap measures larger than the armhole, it must be eased into position. The professional looking sleeve has no excess gathers or pleats at the sleeve cap.

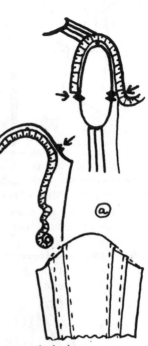

The sleeve cap should measure 1-1/2" larger than the armhole for woolens, rayons, linens and cottons not having a permanent press finish, and about 1" larger for polyesters and those fabrics with a permanent press finish.

To measure the sleeve cap, stand the tape measure on edge and measure between the notches on the stitching line. Do the same on the garment armhole between the notches. (a) (The distance below the notches is the same on both garment and sleeve, so there is no need to measure the lower part.) Remove any excess in sleeve cap by taking several small tucks between the notches and shoulder dot.

Extra fullness is also found in the sleeve cap area when one has a more triangular shaped upper arm (at shoulder).

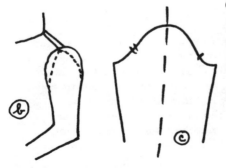

Consequently, there is excess cloth. (b) To eliminate the problem, make a sleeve with a seam down the middle. Slash pattern from middle of wrist to shoulder dot. (c)

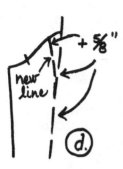

Remove excess at sleeve cap by
making line at an angle. (d)
Add 5/8" seam allowance. This sleeve
still gives fullness at the upper arm
area, yet eliminates excess at the
sleeve cap.

CHECK THE SIZE OF ARMHOLES:

Measure the front and back halves of armholes on both sleeveless garments and
those having sleeves. Compare with the
pattern. If enlarging is necessary,
do so at the bottom of the armhole and also on the sleeve. (a)

UNDERLINING SLEEVES:

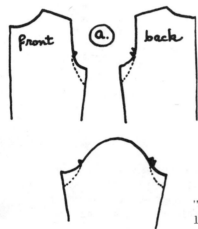

1. Use lightweight under-
    lining such as SiBonne!
    crisp or soft finish, or
    soft Siri (with heavier
    fabric), cut on bias.

2. Follow instructions for
    pinning and folding given
    in the section entitled
    "The Underlined Dress", pages
    19-23.

EASING CAP OF SLEEVE:

1. Stitch one row of long machine stitches (6 per inch) at 5/8"
    from edge of sleeve cap between notches. There's less chance
    of breaking this thread if either silk or nylon thread is used in
    the bobbin, and this thread is pulled for easing.

2. Measure distance between shoulder
    seam and each notch on bodice
    pattern pieces. Mark same
    distance with plastic-head
    pins on shoulder board or
    tailor's ham. (b) Reverse
    pins for opposite sleeve.

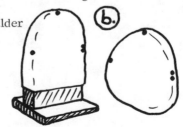

3. Pin sleeve to shoulder board matching shoulder dot and notches.
(Underarm seams of sleeve should not be stitched yet.) Pull
easing thread from both directions until notches match pins
on shoulder board or ham. (c)

4. Steam (iron held about 1/4" above sleeve fabric) seam
allowance to shrink fullness from cap of sleeve. Let dry.
Repeat until sleeve cap is smooth. (If you don't have a steam
iron, then use wool presscloth--sprinkle water on surface.)

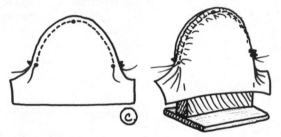

5. Remove from board or ham. Stitch underarm seams, and
hem. Matching notches and dots, install sleeves.

FINISH ARMHOLE:

After sleeves are in, machine stitch second row about 3/8" from
edge in the lower part of the armhole--between notches. Trim
seam allowance to stitching. Trim upper seam allowance to
1/2". (This eliminates the need to clip seam allowances which
will weaken the seam.) (d)

Raglan Sleeves

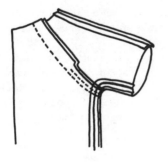

--This sleeve is recommended for fabrics having a permanent press finish and those which are difficult to shrink or ease without excess gathers and puckers.

--For a more comfortable fit, stitch underarm seams of both sleeve and garment separately. Then stitch sleeve in position--like setting in a sleeve. Press open seam. Trim lower part like set-in sleeve.

Gussets

--Gussets are the diamond or triangular shaped pieces set into the underarm area of garments where the sleeve is cut in one piece with the body section. It makes the garment fit well and provides extra freedom of movement. Garments having gussets can fit closer to the body than those without (less ease is needed).

Needed: 4 pieces fabric to face slashes--2" wide and 5" long.
(Use lightweight lining fabric, such as SiBonne! or Siri.)
2 squares of fashion fabric (5-1/4").

1. Mark 4" slashes on each sleeve from underarm toward neck.

2. Fold facing strips lengthwise and press crease through centers. Match creaseline to slash marking, right sides together.

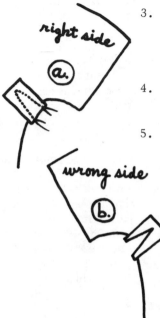

3. Stitch (20 stitches per inch), beginning at edge 1/4" from slash line, tapering to a point. Make one stitch across point, then stitch down other side. (a)

4. Slash on line. (b) Turn facings back to wrong sides. Press.

5. Pin and stitch underarm seams of bodice and sleeve. Press open.

6. Slip gusset square under opening. Pin in place from right side, placing edges of opening 5/8" from edge of square.

7. Topstitch close to faced edge of opening from right side. (c)

Changing a regular sleeve to a full sleeve...

To make a full sleeve, more cloth is needed in the lower sleeve-- not at the top.
(For a puff sleeve, then more would be added to the entire width of the sleeve or just to the sleeve cap.)

Slash sleeve from bottom to top edge--to the solid dark line, but not through. Slash four times. Spread pattern the needed amount at the bottom. Nothing is added to the sleeve cap. Connect disconnected parts of the lower edge for the new cutting line.

Full sleeve... elasticized at wrist

Excellent to use with voiles and chiffons!

Make a full sleeve (as described above) and add 6" extra length to bottom to create a layered puff effect. Stitch a casing to the sleeve 6" from bottom edge. Insert elastic, an inch smaller than arm. Hem sleeve with a narrow handkerchief hem.

When wearing, pull sleeve up so elastic is between wrist and elbow. This creates layered effect.

ROLLED COLLARS:

For both points of the collar to look alike, the undercollar and interfacing should be in two parts and cut on the bias. Thus both sides will be exactly the same grain and shape the same way. (a)

EXTREMELY POINTED COLLARS:

In order to prevent bulk in the point region, yet provide enough support and reinforcement, interfacings must be removed from the point before stitching. Remove about 1 to 1-1/2" in that region. (b)

STITCHING COLLARS AND FACINGS TO THE NECKLINE:

For each side to fit closely to the neck, stitching must be done in the same direction on both halves. So, either stitch from center back to center front or center front to center back on each half, Do not begin at center front and stitch completely around the neck to center front.

a.

remove

b.

CHECK SIZE OF UPPER AND UNDER COLLARS AND LAPELS:

The upper collar should be larger than the under collar to allow for the roll and to prevent the corners from turning up. If there is a rolled lapel, the front facing should be larger than the jacket front above the break-line.

Allow 1/8" extra for dress and shirt weight fabrics, 1/4" for lightweight suitings, and 1/2" for heavier suiting and coating fabrics. Add to the outer edges, tapering to nothing at the center front edge of a collar and the breakline points on the lapel. (a)

TWO-SECTION COLLARS:

Assemble each section. Overlap stitching lines at center front or center back. Stitch by hand or machine to hold together. This eliminates the possibility of one side shifting as the collar is stitched to the garment. (b)

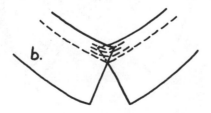

TAILOR'S BLISTER:

To attach the upper and under-collar sections where the upper
collar is cut larger, use the tailor's blister. Pinch a tuck in the
corner about 1-1/2" from the point. The tuck should equal the
added amount--1/8" if 1/8" was added to the collar, etc. Then
match edges of collars and stitch. When ready to turn collar (after
grading seam allowances), remove pin. Excess cloth will return
to point so points of collar will turn under rather than stick out.
(This is also used for rolled lapels where the facing is cut larger
than the garment above the lower break point.) (a)

FASTENING STAND-UP COLLARS:

If hooks and eyes are used for fastening edges of stand-up collars
together, they often unfasten when the garment is worn. Instead,
use snaps. Stitch socket side to one side of collar next to edge.
On the other side, stitch the snap to the edge only in one hole.
This snap will be dangling now. When snapped, the stand-up
collar edges will just meet and still stay fastened! (b)

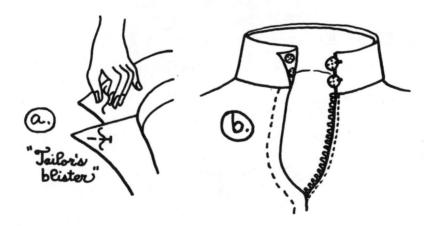

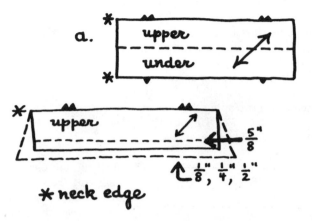

* **neck edge**

IMPROVE THE ROLL OF A ONE-PIECE COLLAR: Make an upper
collar and two under collars. This way, both sides will look alike.

1. Cut the collar in half on the lengthwise fold line. Add 5/8" seam
    allowance plus 1/2" or 1/4" or 1/8"(see "Check Size of Collars")
    to that edge on the upper collar. (a)

2. Cut under collar section in half and add 5/8" to that new center
    back seam you've just created. Also, add 5/8" seam allowance
    to the former "fold" line edge. (b)

(The actual neck edge has not been changed in size. All additions
and changes are being made on the outside edges.)

3. If you have already cut the collar, then plan to stitch the ends
by hand. (c) Sew collar to neckline, but do not finish ends by
machine.

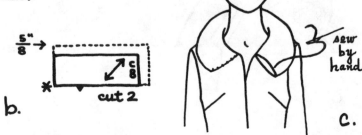

WEDDING RING COLLARS:

--For softer fabrics, substitute a softer look at the neckline for that stand-up collar.

1. Use pattern for stand-up collar.(a)

2. Instead of interfacing the collar, cut a strip of woven lambs-wool * (ARMO-WOOL) cut on the bias 7" and the length of the collar less seam allowances.

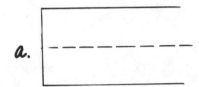

3. Roll the lambswool like a jellyroll from one long side to the other long side until the desired thickness is achieved. Then stitch the edge to the roll. (b)

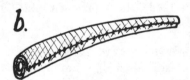

4. Stitch one edge of collar to the garment at the neckline (right sides together). Clip seams. Insert roll of lambswool. Tack to neckline seam.

5. Bring unattached edge of collar over lambswool roll. Slipstitch to neckline seam allowance. Finish ends of collar by hand creating a "round" look. (c)

*For washable garments, use nylon stockings.

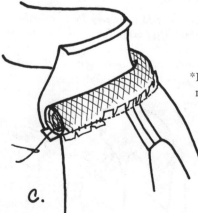

SEWING COLLAR IN V-NECKLINE:

1. Mark point * where seamlines
intersect at neck. Staystitch garment
on seamline using small stitches, taking
one stitch across point. Slash to point.
(a) (*Point is usually deeper than 5/8".)

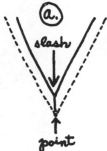

2. When pinning collar to neckline, slip
seam allowance of one end of collar through
slash. (b) Overlap other collar so stitching
line of collar is on stitching line of V-neck. (c)

3. Baste to neckline. Stitch facing in place. Trim seams and
clip.

4. Turn facing back to wrong side; press; understitch.

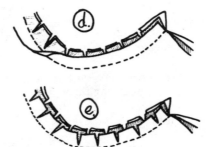

CLIPPING CURVED SEAM ALLOWANCES:

In order for a facing or collar to be smooth it is necessary to clip
the curved areas. Rather than clipping through all thicknesses
in the same places, stagger the clipping, (d).Clip half the layers,
then clip the other layers inbetween. (e)

Facings

ARMHOLE FACINGS:

--For a flat professional appearance, use facings rather than bias tape for sleeveless garments.

1. Trace around front and back armholes, making grainline parallel to that of garment. Make 2" wide. (a)

2. To eliminate bulk at shoulder, make one-piece armhole facing by overlapping shoulder seam allowances of front and back facings. Redraw grainline so it is at a right angle to the shoulder line. (b)

FINISHING THE BOTTOM EDGE OF FACINGS:

1. Edge stitch and zigzag if fabric is firmly woven and bulky. This eliminates the edge from showing on the right side and controls any potential ravelling. (c)

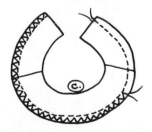

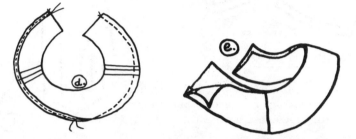

2. Turn under edge and machine stitch in place for a less bulky fabric. Hint, in order to turn the edge smoothly and easily, first stitch by machine where edge will be turned. Then turn on stitching! (d)

3. Face the facing with lightweight lining. This is the nicest looking finish--all raw edges are enclosed. (e) (In fact, use lining for both the facing and facing the facing.)

FINISHING FACING FOR ZIPPER INSTALLATION:

> --Done before stitching zipper. This method is not applicable
> for invisible zippers. It gives a clean finish without excess
> bulk at the top of the zipper.

1. Pin facings to garment at neckline. Before stitching:

For overlap zipper:

> --On right back of dress (underlap side of zipper), fold back
> 1/2" of facing seam allowance on facing. (a) Fold back
> 1/2" of garment seam allowance back on top of facing seam
> allowance. (b)

> --On left back of dress (overlap side of zipper), fold back
> facing seam allowance plus 3/8" (1") on facing. (c) Fold
> back 5/8" seam allowance of garment back on top of facing
> seam allowance. (d)

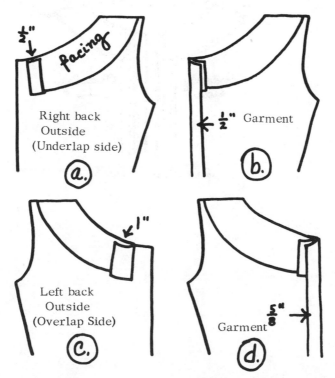

For slot zipper.

   a. On both sides of dress, fold facing seam allowance
      plus 1/4" back on facing. Fold garment seam allowance
      (5/8") on top of facing seam allowance.

2. Stitch through all thicknesses. Clip to stitching; grade seams.

3. Turn to wrong side; press.

4. Follow instructions for inserting zippers on pages

5. Tack facing to zipper tape.

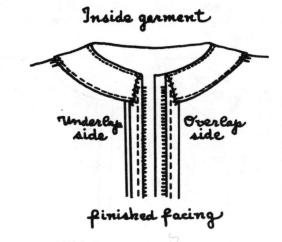

COMBINATION NECK AND ARMHOLE FACING:

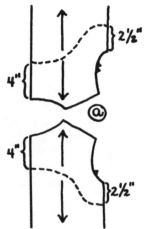

--This eliminates bulk at shoulder area where separate facings would overlap.

--Since most patterns do not give this combination for sleeveless garments, you must make your own pattern.

1. Trace around neck and armholes for front and back bodice, marking grainline. (Exclude bustline darts in underarm or armhole areas by pinning before tracing. Include darts at neckline or shoulder.)

2. Remove bodice pattern pieces. Mark dot on underarm seam 2-1/2" below armhole. Mark dot at center front and center back, 4" below neck edge. Connect lines to make bottom edge of facing. (a) (For a dress with a scooped neck, mark dot about 2" below neck edge at center front or back.)

3. To prevent facing from showing at neck or armhole, make facing less in width at shoulder. Trim 1/4" from armhole of facing at the shoulder, tapering to nothing at armhole notches. (b)

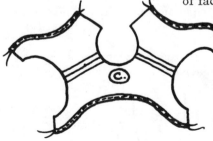

4. Prepare facing by joining shoulder seams only. Press open. Finish bottom edge of facing. (c) (See methods on pages 67 and 68.)

5. Join shoulder seams only on garment, also. Press open. Trim back underlining to stay-stitching.

6. Pin facing section to garment at neckline and armholes; pin on tighter at shoulder area because facing is less in width.

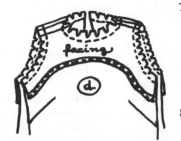

7. Before stitching, pin-fit dress at neck and armholes. Once stitched, this combination facing is more difficult to change. Stitch around neck and armholes through all thicknesses.

8. Grade seams at neckline and armholes; clip curves. Leave seam allowance longest on part of garment receiving the most strain. (At the neck, the dress seam allowance is longest.) (d)

9. Pull two-part section of garment (section that is open at either center front or back) through shoulder opening--between fashion fabric and facing. (e)

10. Press. Understitch.

11. Sew side seams--place right sides of fashion fabric together; do the same for facing.   Make one continuous seam. Press open. Turn down facing. Tack to underarm seam allowance. (f) Or, turn to right side and stitch by machine in crevice where front joined back. (g)

12. Sew center back or front seams. Finish garment.

facing

facing

right side dress

inside - side view

Zippers

There is no "one way" to install
a zipper. And, there is no one type of
zipper that is superior. Your garment
style and fabric will help you decide which
type to purchase.

For lighter weight synthetics, you'll find
the nylon zippers are wise choices because metal zippers
may be too heavy. The invisible zippers are ideal for
inconspicuous closures. When a separating zipper is used
in a garment that will be worn unfastened, the ones with
covered teeth are especially handsome.

When using a separating zipper or regular zipper for a
fly - front application, cover the zipper tape with self-colored
lace. The exposed tape and machine stitching will not be noticed,
especially when jackets are worn unzipped.

Where a long separating zipper is suggested for the bodice
of a two piece dress, you can substitute two shorter ones. Insert
one at the center back neckline and one in the left side seam so it
opens from the hem edge.

A special zipper foot is required for the invisible zippers,
and a regular zipper foot is suggested for installing a professional
looking zipper.

Preshrink zippers according to instructions on page 9.

I. EASY "OVERLAP" INSTALLATION:

1. Preshrink zippers.

2. Stitch seam to notch or dot marking zipper opening.
   Staystitch seam allowances in zipper area.

3. Working from the outside of the garment, turn under
   1/2" of seam allowance on right side of garment
   (underlap side of zipper). Turn under 5/8" seam
   allowance on left side of garment. (a)

4. Place zipper under opening with tab and teeth up. Pin
   right side close to zipper teeth. Top stitch from outside
   of garment close to teeth. (b)

5. Turn to wrong side of garment. Stitch edge of zipper to
   edge of other seam allowance by machine--1/8" to 1/4"
   from edge. (c)

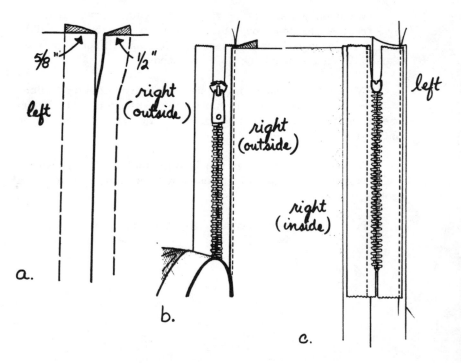

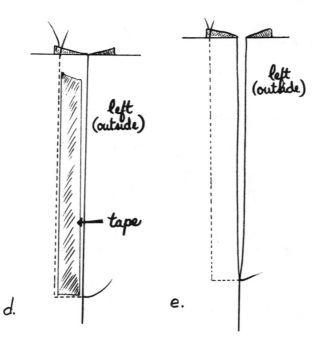

d.   e.

6. Turn back to outside of garment. Topstitch overlap side
   through all thicknesses between 3/8" to 1/2" from fold.
   Use cellophane tape as guide when stitching to insure
   even width from edge of fold. (d)

II. FOR KNITS OR STRETCHY FABRICS:

   --follow steps 1, 2 and 3 -- preceeding page.

4. On overlap side (where 5/8" seam allowance was turned
   under), topstitch by machine or hand through fashion
   fabric and seam allowance (3/8" to 1/2" from fold and
   across bottom to seam). (e)

5. Slip zipper under opening. Follow steps 4 and 5 --
   preceeding page.

III. "SLOT" METHOD INSTALLATION: (stitching equal distance from zipper teeth)

1. Preshrink zippers.

2. Stitch seam to notch or dot marking zipper opening. Staystitch seam allowance in zipper area.

3. Above notch, turn under 5/8" seam allowance and press.

4. On wrong side, place zipper face down on seam allowance 1/8" from edge of seam allowance. Pin to seam allowance. (a)

5. Stitch zipper tape to seam allowance by machine next to zipper teeth. (b)

6. Turn to outside of garment. Hand-pick or topstitch 1/4" from folded edge on both sides of zipper teeth (through all thicknesses). Stitch from bottom to top. Use cellophane tape as a guide when stitching to insure even width. (c)

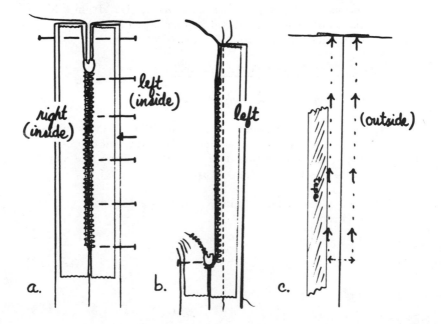

right (inside)   left (inside)   left   (outside)

a.   b.   c.

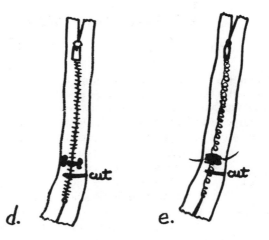

IV. TO SHORTEN ZIPPERS:

   1. For metal zippers, sew "eye" from hook and eye across
       teeth near bottom of zipper. (d) Cut excess length with
       wire cutters.

   2. For nylon zippers, overcast across teeth at desired
       place. Cut excess length with scissors. (e)

Waistbands

I. FACING INSTEAD OF BAND:

This is undoubtedly the most comfortable finish
for the waistline because it just comes to the
waist and is not binding. Often patterns will
suggest the use of grosgrain here. It, however,
is a straight piece of ribbon and will not fit as
smoothly as it should
without pleats and tucks--
which add to the bulk at the waistline. Also,
a bias strip does not fit as smoothly.

1. Make your facing pattern by pinning
    waistline darts in pattern pieces; then
    trace around top edge of pattern. (a)
    Make 2-2-1/2" wide with straight
    grainline at center front and back. (b)

2. Don't forget to interface waist using
    facing pattern. This gives more
    support and prevents stretching.

    3. Cut facing from fashion fabric unless
it is bulky. Then select a lighter weight material such as an
underlining or lining fabric.

4. Finish bottom edge of facing. (See page 67-68.)

5. Stitch facing to waist after side seams and darts have been
    stitched on garment. If skirt is lined, attach lining before
    facing is applied. Check page 69 for information on finishing
    facing for zipper installation.

6. Grade seams, leaving skirt seam allowance the longest. Under-
    stitch. Tack facing to seam allowances at sides and back by
    hand, or stitch by machine in seamline crevice--so stitches
    are concealed.

(Note: Top of skirt should equal waist size to fit smoothly.)

II. BIAS-CUT BAND:

--This band is also comfortable and flexible since
it is cut on the bias. It is also recommended for
a short-waisted person.

1. For the length of regular bands, see "III--The Grosgrain
Backed Band." Cut bias band 1" to 2" shorter (1" if
material is more firmly woven; 2" if fabric is extremely
stretchy or loosely woven). For width, cut 3-1/2" wide.

2. Sew darts in skirt; install zipper; attach lining. Sew a
piece of pre-shrunk seam tape to waistline to prevent
stretching. Tape should equal your waist measurement
plus 1" ease.)

3. Place bias piece on right side of garment--stitch at 5/8"
from edge. Do not trim--seam allowance serves as
interfacing. (a)

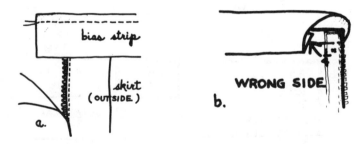

4. Turn bias back to wrong side, covering seam allowance. (b)

5. Turn under bottom edge of bias strip and pin to skirt so
1/4" of bias extends below stitching line. (b)

6. From right side of garment, stitch in the crevice--crack
   where band joins the skirt. (c) Since there is a 1/4"
   extension of bias, it will be caught with this stitching.
   Thus, hand-stitching will be eliminated and the band
   is more securely anchored.

7. For a more professional look, finish ends by hand.
   Rather than making buttonholes in band, use "skirt
   fasteners" and a snap to fasten. (d)

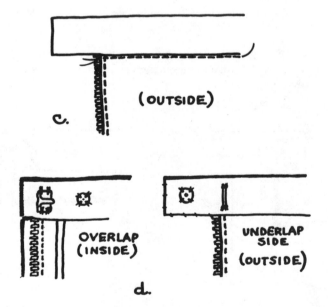

III. GROSGRAIN-RIBBON BACKED BAND:

--In this case, the grosgrain not only serves as the
back of the band, but also eliminates the need for
a piece of interfacing. It is excellent with bulky
fabrics.

1. LENGTH OF BAND:

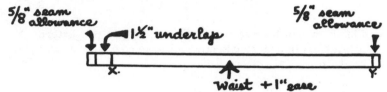

2. Purchase grosgrain ribbon 1/4" wider than width of finished
band. Preshrink.

3. Width of fashion fabric band should include two seam allowances.

4. Working from right side of fashion fabric, overlap grosgrain
on band 5/8" from edge. Pin and stitch. Trim this seam
allowance to 1/4". (a)

5. Pin band to skirt waistline with right sides together after
zipper and linings are installed. Pin from skirt side,
beginning with points "x" and "y" on band. Ease skirt to
band.

6. Stitch with permanent stitching on skirt side at 5/8" from edge.
Press seam allowance toward band. Trim waistband seam
allowance to 3/8".

7. Fold grosgrain back over seam allowance to wrong side. Pin.
(b)

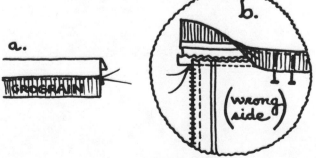

8. On right side, machine stitch in crevice (where skirt joins band) to catch grosgrain permanently. (c)

9. Finish ends of band by hand. Clip grosgrain that extends below band in underlap section. Turn under and stitch by hand. (d)

IV. ELASTIC CASING:

--This form of waistband eliminates the need for zippers
and darts; thus, it is fast. It is not recommended if
the waist is very small in comparison to the hips.

1. When cutting garment, add twice the elastic width to the
   pattern at the waist plus seam allowance. (a)

2. Eliminate darts; double check to see that waist measure is the
   same as hips. This is necessary so the garment can be pulled
   over hips.

3. Sew garment side seams, etc. Turn under seam allowance at
   top of skirt or slacks. Press.

4. Stitch this folded edge to waist by machine, leaving a one-
   inch opening. Use polyester, silk or nylon thread.

5. Preshrink elastic. Cut waist measurement less one-inch in
   length.

6. Thread elastic through casing using safety pin. Overlap ends
   (b); either stitch by hand or machine. Slipstitch one-inch
   opening in casing to garment.

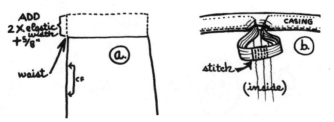

7. If wide elastic is used, stitch through casing and elastic using straight stitch or "s" stitch. Pull waistline so fabric and elastic are both stretched as you sew. This permits stretching later, yet eliminates the problem of the elastic twisting inside the casing. (c)

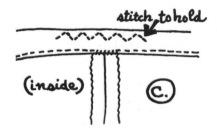

Belts

BELT WITH BUCKLE:

1. To determine width of belt for buckle, measure opening. Make belt 1/8" less in width. (d)

2. Cut belt 6" longer than waistline measurement for a belt 1" wide. (For any belt over 1" wide, add 1/2" in length for every additional inch in width.)

3. Attach cloth carrier 1-1/2" from buckle. (e)

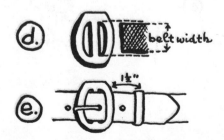

BELT BACKING:

Because belt backing is available only in a limited number of colors, enclose it in the belt rather than backing the belt.

1. Cut fashion fabric twice the width of the backing plus seam allowances.

2. Fold the belt in the lengthwise direction so edges are matched -- right sides together.

3. Seam the lengthwise side and one end using a scant seam allowance. Trim seams; turn to right side. Press.

4. Cut belt backing where the buckle will be attached to eliminate bulk.

5. Insert backing. Attach buckle. (If prong is to be used, make a buttonhole where the prong will be slipped through the belt. Also, use small machine buttonholes for the eyes.

SOFT, CRUSHABLE BELT:

1. To give and keep a soft appearance, fashion fabric and interfacing are cut on the bias; 6" wide
   waist +10" for length.

2. Cut interfacing half width and 6" shorter than belt. Fasten in position.

3. Seam belt with right sides together. Trim seams. Turn.

4. Press; attach buckle.

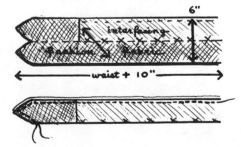

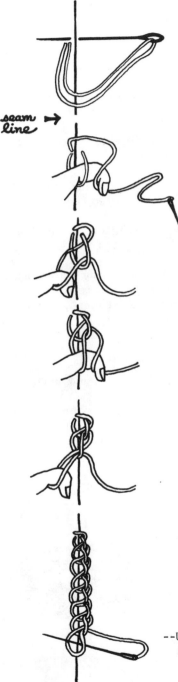

seam line →

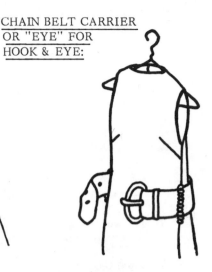

CHAIN BELT CARRIER OR "EYE" FOR HOOK & EYE:

1. Make stitch in fabric on right side. In place of pulling tight, leave loop.

2. Through loop, pull thread with finger, holding securely to other end with left hand.

3. Original loop will tighten into chain stitch; pull thread through new loop and tighten into chain stitch.

4. When chain reaches desired length, pull thread through. This will automatically knot chain.

5. Push needle through cloth to wrong side. Fasten with several stitches. Tie knot.

--Use buttonhole twist or several strands of thread.

Hems

SUGGESTED WIDTHS:

Slim skirts	2-1/2" to 3"
A-line skirts	1-1/2" to 2"
Circle	1" to 1-1/4"
Sheer circle	Handkerchief width

EASING HEM TO SKIRT -- before applying hem finish

(One true sign of a "home-made" garment is the hem with pleats
at the top edge - visible from the right side of the garment.
Instead, hems should be eased to the inside skirt, so they appear
smooth on the outside.)

1. Use a long machine basting stitch to distribute fullness at hem
   edge so hem fits inside of skirt smoothly. This eliminates the
   need for tucks or pleats at the top edge.

> --Baste an A-line skirt from side seam to side seam.
> (a)
> --Baste a circle skirt from center front or back to
>   each side seam. (b)

2. Pull easing thread from both directions in each section. To
   prevent thread from breaking while pulling, use either nylon or
   silk in bobbin. Pull that thread.

3. Once hem is eased to skirt, steam press to shrink excess fullness. Then apply hem finishes such as seam tape, lace or
   Hong Kong finish.

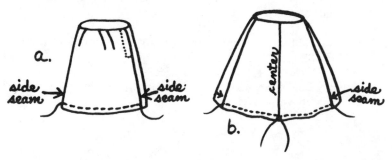

SOFTENED OR DEFINED HEMLINES???

--Today interfacings are being incorporated in hems to either
soften the edge and give a feminine look or define the shape so a
garment encircles rather than clings.

1. Cut interfacing strip on the bias--long enough to reach around
   the hem. Seam on the straight of grain if necessary to piece.

2. The width depends on finished effect:

   --For a firm hem in lighter weight fabrics, enclose bias strip
   in hem. (Cut it the exact width of the hem.)

   --For a firm hem in heavier fabrics, such as jacket and sleeve
   hems, cut strip of interfacing 1/2" wider than hem. Place
   one edge next to foldline. Stitch bias to hem along top edge
   and 1/2" from fold. (a) Fasten hem to garment. (b) (By
   extending the interfacing beyond the hem, it acts as a cushion
   so hem edge won't show on the outside.)

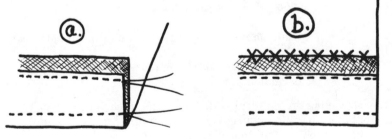

   --For a softer, rolled hem, interfacing is extended beyond the
   fold so it is actually folded back on itself. (Instructions for
   "softer hems" follow.)

3. Suggested fabrics:

   For washable garments: Formite, Acro, firm Siri or
   soft Siri.

   For dry cleanable garments: Finolight, Lambswool,
   plus above fabrics.

FOR SOFTER HEM: (f or lighter weight garments and those
        without underlining) (a)

1. Cut bias strip 1-1/2' times the hem width.

2. Position bias strip so one edge of strip is next to edge of hem
    and other extends beyond fold.

3. Either hand or machine baste strip to hem 1/2" from top and
    fold.

4. Hem as usual.

FOR SOFTER HEM: (heavier fabrics or underlined garments) (b)

1. Cut bias strip 2" wider than hem.

2. Position bias strip on garment so 1" extends beyond fold into
    hem.* Catchstitch interfacing at top and bottom to underlining.

3. Turn up hem. Hand stitch to interfacing strip. Interfacing
    should extend above hem edge by 1".

(*Baste strip next to fold.)

(For A-line and circular skirts, cut bias strips in sections rather
than one continuous strip. Taper ends of each strip so they are at
the same angle as the skirt. This eliminates possible buckling
at the top edge of the bias strip.)

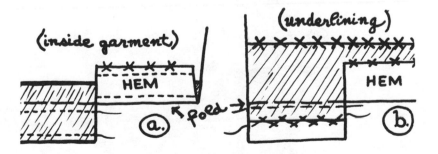

HEMMING WITH A PLEAT:

1. If a garment has a pleat with a seam, leave seam open for about
    7 inches above raw bottom edge. (a)

2. Hem garment. (b) Then stitch open part of seam through finished
    hem. Trim diagonally at bottom corner of seam. Overcast or
    bind seam edge. (c)
    (This is especially helpful for bulky fabrics and polyester double
    knits.)

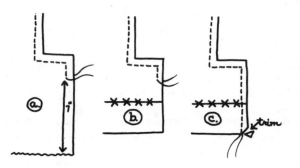

STITCHING PLEATS DOWN:

   --This may be necessary if bulky, polyester knits, or
   permanent press fabrics are being used. Edge stitch both
   the under-fold and outer fold. (d)

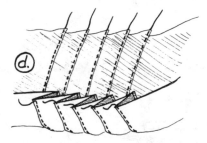

HANGING PLEATS IN GARMENTS:

Many garments today include pleats. You'll see them in jackets, coats, and princess style dresses. It may be a side pleat (pressed in one direction) or an inverted pleat (two equal folds turned toward each other).

If there is no support or way to anchor the top edge of the pleat without stitches showing on the outside of the garment, then --
--attach preshrunk seam binding to the top edge of the pleat. Attach other end of tape to waistline or neckline seam. (a)

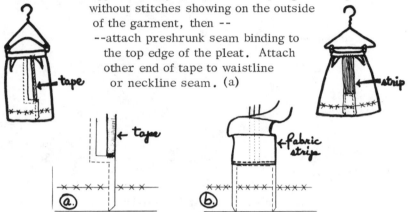

--Cut underlining fabric (on straight of grain) the width of the pleat. Attach one end to the pleat, the other to the waistline or neckline seam. (b)

PLEATED SKIRT AND OVERBLOUSE:

--To eliminate bulk at waistline, make a smooth "upper skirt" from underlining fabric and attach pleats at hipline or one-two inches above bottom edge of overblouse.

HONG KONG FINISH:

This bound hem finish can be used for seams and facing edges. It's great with fabrics that ravel excessively. For an individual custom look, use contrasting colors for the binding.

1. Cut bias strips of lightweight lining fabric about 1-1/4" wide. If piecing is necessary, seam strips on grain, or make continuous bias strip. (Instructions follow.)

2. Ease hem edge to skirt.

3. Place bias strip face down on right side of fashion fabric with raw edges together. (a)

4. Machine stitch at 1/4". Trim to 1/8". (b)

5. Turn bias strip over trimmed raw edge to wrong side forming a casing 1/8" wide on the outside of the hem. Press. Secure with pins. (c)

6. On right side of fabric, top stitch by machine close to edge where casing joined hem (in crevice). Slipstitch hem to underlining of garment. (d)

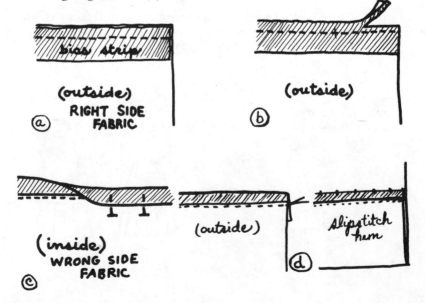

(outside)
RIGHT SIDE
FABRIC
ⓐ   bias strip

(outside)
ⓑ

(inside)
WRONG SIDE
FABRIC
ⓒ

(outside)

slipstitch hem
ⓓ

CUTTING A CONTINUOUS BIAS STRIP: (Save time--quicker than
    sewing together individual strips of bias.)

1. Cut a square of fabric (lining preferred) diagonally into two
   pieces. (a)

2. Join one set of straight sides that are opposite in the square. (b)
   Press open seam. (c)

3. Before joining other set of straight sides, mark the desired
   width of strips parallel to bias. These markings will be used
   later as guides for cutting. (d)

4. Join second set of sides, but INSTEAD of matching top and
   bottom edges, match row #1 at one end and row #2 at the other
   end, right sides together. Stitch and press open the seam.
   (You will have an extension above and below the major strip.)
   (e)

5. Begin cutting on marked line at one end where there is the
   extension. Continue to cut in a circular manner to make one
   continuous strip of bias. (e)

(All stitching should be about 20 stitches per inch.)

a.

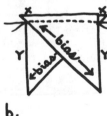

b.

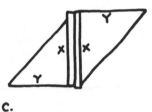

c.

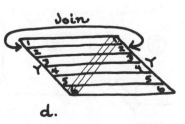

d.

cut

Pockets

I. UNLINED, SQUARE PATCH POCKET:

1. Cut pocket with 1-1/2" extension for facing at top edge. (a)

2. Finish lower edge of facing--zigzag, overcast or turn under and stitch.

3. Fold upper facing so right side of facing is next to right side of pocket. (b)

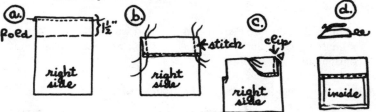

4. On both sides, stitch from top edge to bottom of facing at 5/8" from edge. (b) Trim seam; cut diagonally at corners. (c) Turn facing back to wrong side. Press. (d)

5. Press under seam allowance on other two sides and bottom.

6. Miter corners:
   --Fold diagonally across corners where seam allowances cross. Press. (e)
   --Trim part of this triangle--1/4" from diagonal fold. (f)
   --Turn under 5/8" seam allowances from both sides. Press; slipstitch by hand to hold permanently. (g)

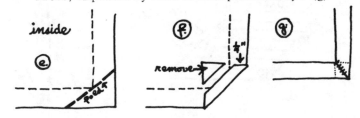

7. Topstitch or slipstitch (by
   hand) pocket to garment.

8. Suggested stitching patterns
   for pocket stays--at upper
   corners: (h)

II. <u>LINED, CURVED PATCH POCKET:</u>

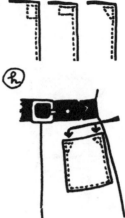

1. Even if pattern does not suggest
   lining, plan to line to achieve
   a smooth rounded edge.

2. Cut lining 1-1/4" longer than
   end of facing (i)

3. With right sides together, stitch
   upper edge of lining to edge of facing at 5/8", leaving a
   one-inch opening in the middle. (j) Press seam open.

4. Match outer edges of lining and pocket. Stitch. Stagger
   seam; and cut notches from curved edges. (k)

5. Reverse pocket by pulling through one-inch opening so
   pocket is right-side-out. Press. (l)

6. Slip-stitch opening. Stitch to garment.

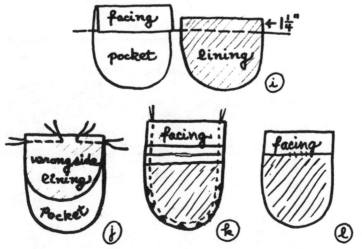

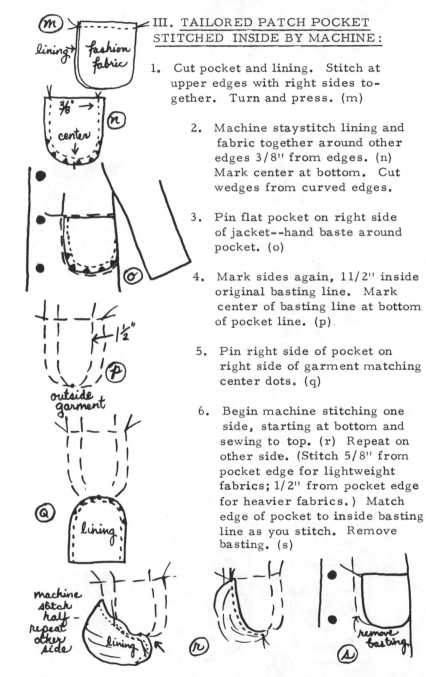

III. TAILORED PATCH POCKET STITCHED INSIDE BY MACHINE:

1. Cut pocket and lining. Stitch at upper edges with right sides together. Turn and press. (m)

2. Machine staystitch lining and fabric together around other edges 3/8" from edges. (n) Mark center at bottom. Cut wedges from curved edges.

3. Pin flat pocket on right side of jacket--hand baste around pocket. (o)

4. Mark sides again, 11/2" inside original basting line. Mark center of basting line at bottom of pocket line. (p)

5. Pin right side of pocket on right side of garment matching center dots. (q)

6. Begin machine stitching one side, starting at bottom and sewing to top. (r) Repeat on other side. (Stitch 5/8" from pocket edge for lightweight fabrics; 1/2" from pocket edge for heavier fabrics.) Match edge of pocket to inside basting line as you stitch. Remove basting. (s)

MEET THE

 Special Edition

On Two Opposing Teams --
SEWING AND PRESSING vs.
WASH DAY AND IRONING

Pressing is an art...an integral part of any garment's construction. You MUST press as you sew to achieve a professional look! Over-pressing gives that "old and worn" appearance. Under-pressing gives a "home-made" look. Pressing involves an up-and-down motion while ironing means sliding the iron over the fabric's surface. Ironing flattens the fibers and gives a glazed appearance.

Characteristics of a well-pressed garment---

No signs of pin or thread basting imprints on outside.
Garment is free from shine and iron marks.
Darts are smooth and rounded at point end--no dimples.
Seams are smooth.
No creases down the center of sleeves in women's suits, coats or better dresses.

Editorial

Pressing techniques and pressing equipment are as important as your sewing techniques. Poor pressing habits may actually press wrinkles in the garment instead of removing them. Organize your pressing and sewing. Locate pressing equipment close to the machine. When pressing, let the garment dry before moving it--otherwise it could stretch when moved.

WHEN TO PRESS--
    --to flatten seams, design and fitting lines.
    --to build shape into a garment, especially curved areas.

How to Press

1. Use an up-and-down motion. (a)

2. Press curved areas over curved surfaces such as tailor hams or mitts. (b)

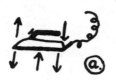

3. First, press darts as stitched, thus forming a crease from the outside edge to the point. (This eliminates having to use excess pressure to flatten darts--imprints are less apt to show on the outside of the garment.) Then, press vertical darts toward either center back or center front, and press horizontal darts down. (c)

4. Each seam should be pressed before it is crossed with another.

5. Each garment section should be pressed before it is joined to another. Press each section completely.

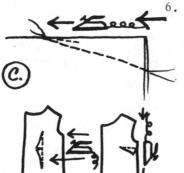

6. Press seams open * unless other- wise directed. Waistline seams are usually pressed up toward the bodice, and armhole seams are pressed into the sleeves. (*By pressing seams flat first, the ten- sion of stitches is equalized and yarns that were distorted by the needle straighten.)

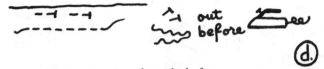

(d.)

7. Remove pins and basting threads before pressing--they will make indentations that are difficult to remove. (d) If basting must be done, silk thread is a better choice than cotton for basting. It's smooth and leaves less of a mark.

8. Use a white vinegar and water solution (half of each) on center folds of fabric to remove the crease line.

9. Press side seams after garment has been fitted. Once some fabrics are creased, the creases are difficult to remove should you need to refit the garment.

10. Never press woolens or linens completely dry.

11. Hang garments on well-padded hangers to complete drying. (e)

12. Avoid ripples in the hem by pressing from the fold edge up to the hem edge. (f)

13. Press with the grainline. (g)

14. Using a clothes brush, brush the surface of soft woolens while damp to raise the nap. Steam cloth, then brush.

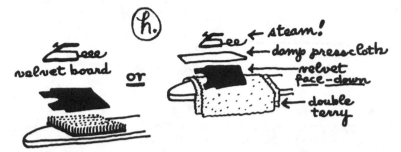

15. A velvet board is suggested for pressing velvets and velveteens.
    If you do not have access to one, then use double pieces of
    terrycloth on the ironing board. Place velvet face-down on
    towels. Use a dampened press cloth on the wrong side. Steam,
    but do not place the weight of the iron on the cloth. (h)

16. For additional moisture, do not saturate a press cloth. Instead,
    spray moisture on the surface of the press cloth. (i)

17. Another piece of wool makes an excellent press cloth for
    woolens. It not only helps to raise the nap of the fashion fabric
    and keep it new looking, but it releases moisture more evenly
    and slowly.

18. Distilled water is suggested for steam irons; however, it is
    not necessary for the press cloth.

19. Do not use the weight of the iron for pressure. Hold the iron
    in your hand. When pressure is needed, use a clapper. With
    today's heat sensitive fabrics, the soleplate indentation is
    found when the iron is used for weight.

20. Even though your iron is equipped with a fabric guide, it is
    wise to test the temperature on a scrap of fabric first. For
    heat sensitive fabrics, also use a dry press cloth between the
    iron and fabric. (j)

SOAPING SEAMS --

To create a flat, thin front edge on a woolen coat or suit, soap the seams where the facing joins the coat.

Stagger seam allowances of the coat and facing; press seams open. Moisten bar of Ivory (100% pure soap)*; rub opened seam until a white soap film appears.

Turn facing to wrong side of garment. Press with steam using press cloth, then clapper. The steam and heat will melt the soap and force it between the woolen fibers. Consequently, the seam allowances will stay together. Do not press directly on soaped seam.

Understitch, if possible.

* Many soaps today contain facial creams and deodorants. The small bars of Ivory provided in motel and hotel rooms are ideal-- easy to hold and use.

EXTRA STEAM --

The new "hand steam wand" --portable appliance - is not only excellent for eliminating wrinkles in clothes but also great for sewing. Use it where you don't want to use a press cloth for additional moisture. And, you'll eliminate the possibility of napped fabrics becoming matted. This extra steam is helpful in shrinking the fullness from sleeve caps and hems.

Pressing Equipment

Pressing is a chore without proper
equipment. These pressing tools
are extremely helpful in creating
a professional looking garment:

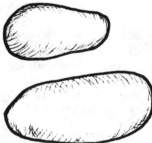

1. Tailor's Ham--used for blocking
   and shaping curved areas such as
   darts and princess seams. Pin
   curved area to ham using straight
   pins while steaming. Let dry on
   ham. Use clapper if additional
   pressure is needed.

2. Sleeve Board--used to press
   seams and construction details
   that could not be placed
   smoothly on an ironing
   board. It looks like a
   miniature-size ironing
   board.

3. Clapper--used as extra pressure to flatten seams, darts, etc. Steam fabric; then place clapper on seam or dart. Hold several minutes. The combination of moisture, heat and pressure (all working together by holding the clapper in one place) will flatten seams.
DO NOT POUND OR BEAT FABRIC.

4. Point presser --used for pressing points of collars, revers and inside seams.

5. Seam board--replaces strips of paper often placed between seam allowances to prevent an imprint from showing on the right side. Because of the rounded edge, the iron only has contact with the seamline and will not press the seam allowance against the outer garment.

6. Seam roll--a cushion used for pressing sleeves and small detail areas. One can improvise by covering several rolled magazines with cloth.

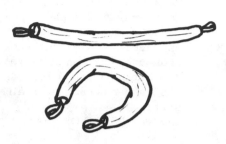

7. Collar Roll--used for shaping the roll in collars and lapels. To use, insert a ribbon in the loops, and tie so curve resembles neckline. Pin collar to roll with breakline on outer edge of inside curve of collar roll. Steam. Let dry. Repeat.

8. Shoulder Board--used for shrinking fullness from cap of sleeve before sleeve is set in garment. Mark a line (thread or pencil) 1-1/4" back from padded edge of shoulder board. Measure distance on paper bodice pattern piece between shoulder dot and notches on armhole of garment. Mark same distance on shoulder board using plastic-head pins. (Use a single pin for the shoulder dot and single notch; use two pins for the double notch.) Run an easing thread (6 stitches per inch) 5/8 inch from the edge of the sleeve cap, between the notches. Pin sleeve to shoulder board, matching notches and shoulder dot. Pull easing thread until sleeve fits shoulder board. Distribute fullness. Steam (with iron about 1/4" above cloth) seam allowance to remove fullness. Let dry. Steam again until sleeve cap is smooth. Then, sew underarm seams of sleeve, hem, and insert in garment.

$\mathcal{B}\text{uttons}$

1. Buttons are always stitched on the center front or center back lines.

2. Buttonholes (horizontal--at right angles to center front or back) begin 1/8" beyond the center front line toward the front edge. (a) Vertical buttonholes would be on either the center front or center back lines. (b)

3. One buttonhole should be across the bustline to avoid gapping. Respace other buttonholes accordingly. (a)

4. There should be 1/2" of fabric extending beyond the button when the garment is buttoned. And, 1/2" above the top button. (c)

If you change the size of button and not purchase the size suggested on the pattern envelope, then you must adjust the pattern before cutting fashion fabric.

--Beyond buttonhole, allow radius of button plus 1/2".
   (For a 1-1/2" button, there should be 1-1/4" of fabric beyond end of buttonhole.)

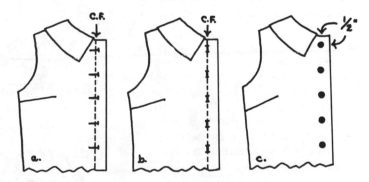

1. Use special "button and carpet" thread. It's
    extra heavy and strong. Or, wax several strands
    of heavy-duty mercerized cotton thread
    or silk thread using bee's wax.

2. Buttons should have a shank in order
    to rest on the surface of the buttonhole
    and be easy to use. The length of the
    shank is determined by the thickness
    of the fabric.

--For a button with a small shank,
place a bobby pin (toothpick or match)
between button and fabric. (a) Sew
on button as usual over bobby pin.
Remove bobby pin, etc. and wind thread
around attaching thread several times.
(b) Then tie knot. Take several small
stitches under button. Cut thread. (c)

--For a "sew-through" button, place
toothpick, etc. on top button after
thread has been brought up through one
hole in button. (d) Stitch on button as
usual over bobby pin. Remove bobby-
pin, and wind thread around attaching
thread. Tie knot. Take several
small stitches under button. Cut
thread.

3. Prevent button from being pulled out
    on heavy garments by sewing a
    small "stay-button" on the wrong
    side of the garment directly
    under the button. (e)

To determine length of buttonhole...

--Measure diameter plus thickness of buttons. (b) For
example; for a round button, 1" in diameter and 1/8"
thick, the buttonhole should be 1-1/8" long.

Exceptions: Ball shaped, square, cloth covered, and odd
shaped buttons. For these, slash fabric until button
slips through easily. Then, measure slash length.

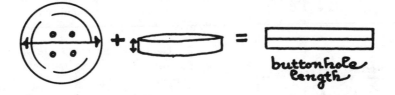

Perfect Bound Buttonholes
...windowpane method...

This method is easy to do and gives a professional looking bound buttonhole with no bulk and a beautiful finish with any type fabric.

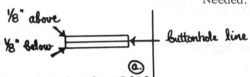

¹⁄₈" above
¹⁄₈" Below
Buttonhole line
ⓐ.

Needed: Pieces of matching lining, cut on bias; one per buttonhole--1-1/2" longer than buttonhole and 2" wide.

Pieces of fashion fabric, 2" wide and 1-1/4" longer than buttonhole for lips; two per buttonhole.

Directions:

1. Mark buttonhole rectangles (length and width of finished buttonhole) on interfacing. (a) If hair canvas is used, replace rectangle behind buttonhole with rectangle of cotton or rayon slightly longer and wider than buttonhole. (Or, catchstitch rectangular hole to underlining.) (b)

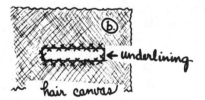

ⓑ
← underlining
hair canvas

2. Center lining rectangle on outside of garment over buttonhole markings. Pin in place.

3. On interfacing side, stitch through all thicknesses following rectangle lines, using 20 stitches per inch. (c)   (Begin and end on side of rectangle, not at points.)

bias lining
ⓒ.
fashion fabric

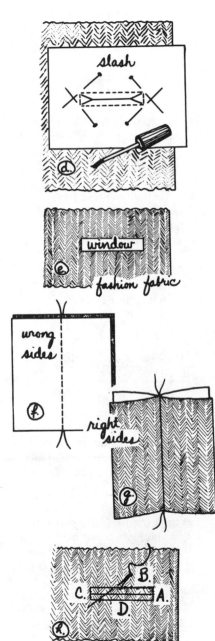

4. Cut through center of rectangle to within 1/4" of each end; slash diagonally to corners. (Use straight pins at corners to prevent scissor from clipping through stitching.) (d)

5. Paint slash with clear finger-nail polish to prevent ravelling. (Plan to use on all fabrics except acetate.)

6. Pull bias patch through slash to form a window--lining serves as facing. Press, making certain lining doesn't show on right side. (e)

PREPARE "LIPS" FOR WINDOWS:

7. Combine two pieces of fashion fabric with right sides together. Machine baste through center in lengthwise direction. (f) (If fabric ravels, cut these pieces on bias. Also, it gives a decorative effect with plaids and stripes. If fabric is loosely woven, back strips with iron-on interfacing.) Press open. (g)

8. Pin lips in position, centering the basted edge in the "window" from the right side of the garment.

9. Working from the right side, slip stitch lips to window along lengthwise sides--"b" and "d". (h)

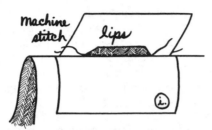

10. If corded buttonhole is desired, thread needle and run cording or yarn through lips now. Then stitch lips to window edge at ends of rectangle--"a" and "c".

11. For extra reinforcement, turn back fashion fabric and machine stitch lips to edge of window. (i)

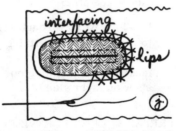

12. Remove basting from center of lips. Grade down all edges on wrong side so none are the same width. The outermost piece (closest to outside of garment) should be the widest. Catch-stitch to interfacing. (j)

FINISH FACING BEHIND BUTTONHOLES:

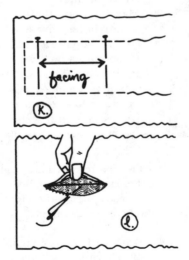

13. Use either another window (follow preceeding instruction) about 1/16" larger than the buttonhole rectangle for the facing; or use a "fish-eye".

14. For the "fish-eye", baste facing around buttonhole area. Stick pin through ends of buttonholes (k) Slash between pins. Turn under cloth at slash to form an oval.(l) Slip-stitch to back of button-hole.

ADAPTING WINDOWPANE BUTTONHOLE FOR MEN'S JACKET OR PANT POCKETS--

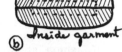

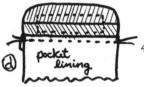

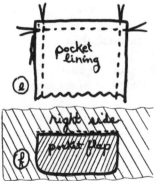

--This is a quick and easy method of installing perfect looking pockets!

1. Interface behind pocket location on wrong side. Mark pocket rectangle (from pattern) on interfacing. Place bias lining on right side. Follow steps 3, 4, 5 & 6 on pages 108-109.

2. Prepare lips (wider) following step 7 on page 109.

3. Pin lips under window so basted seam is centered. Machine topstitch around window opening from right side (through lips, lining, interfacing & fabric). (a-b)

4. Turn under and press seam allowance at one end of pocket lining. (c) Overlap on lower edge of lower lip on wrong side. Stitch. (d)

5. Place upper edge of pocket lining on edge of upper lip. Stitch together. Stitch sides and bottom edges of pocket lining together. (e)

--If pocket has a flap, prepare flap according to directions. Insert from upper side of window either with or in place of the upper lip, during step 3. (f)

HAND-WORKED BUTTONHOLES: These are made last after facing has been stitched to jacket. Mark buttonholes in garment.* Use small paper punch for keyhole at front end of buttonhole. Machine stitch (20 stitches per inch) around buttonhole, close to slash line. Slash. Then stitch by hand using blanket stitch and single strand thread. Make stitch 1/8" deep. Bar tack end using overcast stitch.

*Make in left front for men; right front for women.

Buttonhole Substitutes

Loops

1. Cut bias strips of fashion fabric the desired length and width (to cover cord) plus 3/4" extra for seam allowance.

2. Cut cord twice the bias length. (If 12" are needed, cut cord 24".)

3. Stitch center of cord securely to one end of bias on wrong side.(a)

4. Fold bias back over cord so right side of fabric is against cord and cord is at center of fold . (b)

5. Stitch 1/8" from cord (for lightweight fabric) and 1/4" from cord (for heavy weight fabric).
   Trim seam allowance so one edge is less in width than the other.
   Gently work bias over exposed cord. Grasp end of cord that is being uncovered. Tug! (c) Cut excess cord when uncovered. (d)

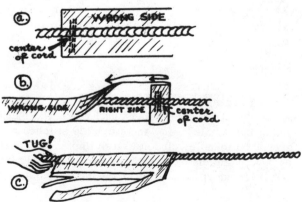

6. Determine length of loops--
   circumference of button plus
   seam allowance.

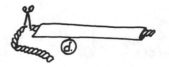

7. Draw size and position of loops
   on either graph or brown paper.
   Baste loops by machine to paper.
   (e)

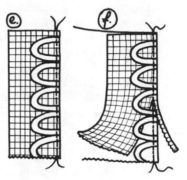

8. Baste paper, with loops to outside of right front, along center
   front edge.   Join facing over
   loops. Tear away paper. (f)
   Stitch again--1/2" from edge.
   (g)

9. Trim seam allowance; understitch. Turn facing to inside
   and press. (h)

(Loops are at center front on
right front--cut pattern at CF
plus seam allowance. Allow
underlap on left side if jacket or
coat is to be worn closed. Or, if
blouse is to show under jacket, cut
left front also at center front plus
seam allowance.)

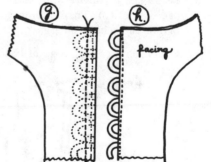

Buttonhole in the band...

These buttonholes are made by applying a band and not stitching the seam at intervals on right front only!

1. If your pattern doesn't feature these buttonholes in a band, then cut right bodice front and facing patterns at center front plus seam allowance. Mark buttonhole intervals on both front and facing.

2. Determine width of band--cut the diameter of the button plus one inch plus two seam allowances (5/8" each). (For a one inch button, cut band 3-1/4" wide.) Cut.

3. Interface front and band.

4. With right sides together, join band to right bodice front and facing, stopping at buttonhole intervals. (a)

5. Press seams open. Catchstitch seams down if fabric does not press flat. (b) Turn facing back to inside right bodice front. Match buttonhole intervals. Slip-stitch to anchor. (c)

6. Press fold at front edge of band. (d)

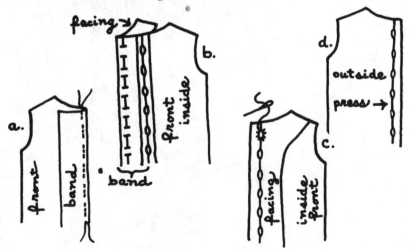

hidden buttons...fly front effect

FOR THE GARMENT WITH A LAPEL

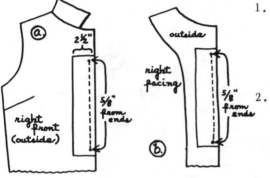

1. Cut two bands from lighter weight fabric (color coordinated). Make band 2-1/2" wide and 1-1/4" longer than the button area.

2. Position bands over button areas on the right front (a) and the right front facing. (b) Stitch, starting and stopping 5/8" from each end. Clip to stitching at each end.

3. Trim seam allowances. Turn band back to inside. Understitch.

4. Turn under ends of band; slipstitch to underlining or interfacing on garment (c) and facing. (d)

5. Make buttonholes through facing and band. (d)

6. Attach facing as directed in pattern instructions. Then topstitch through garment and facing to anchor permanently. Sew flat buttons in position on left front opposite buttonholes. (e)

FOR CARDIGAN STYLE GARMENT:

7. Cut two bands (from lighter weight fabric-- color coordinated) and interfacing. Make 3/4" less in width than facing and the length of the button area, plus seam allowance. (f)

8. Stitch both ends and side closest to front edge; grade seams. Turn to wrong side. Press. (g)

9. Space buttonholes; make by machine in band. Cut open.

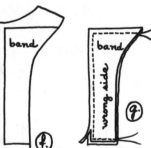

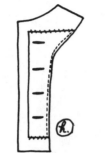

10. Sew band to right front facing at top, bottom and toward curved edge of facing, leaving front edge open. Tack band to facing by hand inbetween button-holes. (h)

11. Apply facing as directed. Topstitch, if desired.

12. After jacket is stitched together, sew flat buttons in place on left front opposite buttonholes. (i)

Decorative Buttons ...
Covered Snaps

When fabrics are loosely woven, it is not possible to always make buttonholes. And when buttons are quite large, the garment looks more professional if buttons are just stitched in place with covered snaps fastening the garment.

1. To cover, purchase large snaps (sizes 2 and 3 are recommended).

2. Cut circle of lining fabric larger than snap. Poke hole in center using sharp scissor point.

3. Run an easing thread around edge of circle. Insert snap. (a)

4. Pull easing thread so cloth covers snap. Secure with several stitches. Tie knot. (b) Trim excess cloth. To prevent ravelling, paint holes with clear fingernail polish.

5. Sew snaps on garment with projection side on right front of garment and socket on left front of garment.

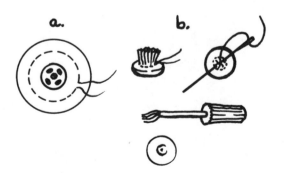

a.   b.

Slot Seams

Slot seams are decorative and can be incorporated in any garment for this special effect.

A contrasting underlap can also be used.

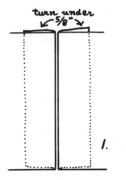

1. Turn under seam allowance on garment. Press.

2. Cut an underlap from fashion fabric 1-1/4" wide and the length of the seam. Straight of grain fabric is best unless the seam is curved -- then use bias. Pin underlap in position under seam allowances.

3. Topstitch from outside of garment 3/8" from folded edges.

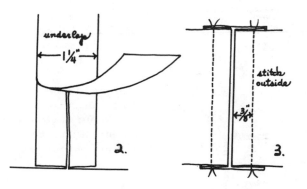

Today's seamstress will find a variety of furs and fake-furs available for garments and trims. Similar techniques would be used for both.

CUTTING: Using a sharp pair of shears or a razor blade, cut only through the skin or backing from the wrong side--not through the long guard hairs. Guard hairs are needed to conceal seaming. Trim pattern. seam allowances to 1/4". Cut out darts, leaving 1/4" for seaming. (a) All pattern pieces should be placed in the same direction (like napped fabrics) so long guard hairs are going down. For a collar, it may be necessary to seam the fur in several places to achieve this look. (b)

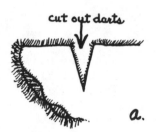

cut out darts

a.

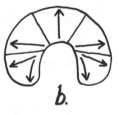

b.

SEWING: Zigzag seams and darts by hand or machine using widest stitch width (#4 on the Bernina machine) and about 10 stitches per inch. Place fur sides together, pushing guard hairs out of the way--in between the two pieces. (c) Zigzag, but do not press. (Steam furs; any heat will "melt" synthetics which are heat sensitive.) Merely, turn to the out-side and brush hairs so seams and darts aren't evident.

For collars, a lining fabric is used for the back rather than a second piece of fur or fake fur to eliminate bulk. This is hand stitched to the collar after the edges of fur have been bound.

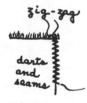

zig-zag

darts
and
seams

c.

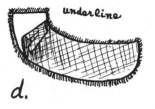

BINDING FUR: To bind a collar or cuff, cut bias strips of lining 1-1/4" wide or pre-shrink packaged cotton bias tape. Press flat. Underline fur with hair canvas, lambswool or cotton flannel. (d) (The underlining serves as a means for anchoring the binding to the collar. You will not be stitching into the skin. For fake furs, the underlining is optional. One can stitch into that backing.)

Pin underlining to fur close to outer edge with pins parallel to the edge. The underlining will be stitched to the collar at the same time the binding is zigzagged in position.

Place binding on fur. Zigzag edge of binding to edge of fur. Turn binding to wrong side so guard hairs are visible from the wrong side. (Otherwise the binding may show on the outside.) Catchstitch binding to underlining or back of fake fur. (e)

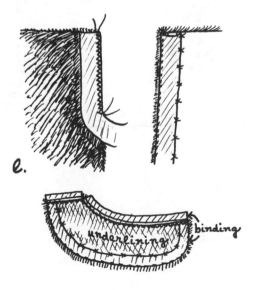

ATTACHING COLLAR TO COAT:

To attach a fur piece to a coat collar, use collar tacks (available
at notions counters) rather than stitching permanently. (f)
It's easier to remove when cleaning the coat.

The collar tacks operate like tie tacks.
The tack half is stitched to the back
side of the fur collar. Place tacks as
close together as necessary. (g)

f.

When attaching the collar, place in
position on the coat and push the tack
through the fabric collar. Squeeze
clutch-back over point until it clasps
securely in position. (h)

h.

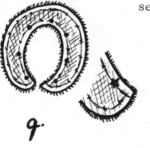

g.

Pants

Today's active woman realizes her wardrobe isn't complete without pants. Due to women's curves, fitting pants is a problem for many. Both the home sewing and manufacturing industries have learned much about the fitting and construction of women's pants from Elsé Tyroler, authoress of Sewing Pants for Women. A number of techniques and tips similar to those set forth in her book have been presented in this chapter with her permission along with many others perfected in my pattern fitting classes.

The correct name for a specific pair of pants is determined by the cut, length and fabric. A general run-down of names is found on the following page.

Any fabric can be used for pants; however, keep in mind that two common problems -- "rump spring" and "baggy knees" -- occur more frequently with some fashion fabrics than with others. To prevent them, underlinings and linings are important. In addition to some woven fabrics, I underline bonded fabrics and lightweight knits as both these fabrics have lots of "give" or stretch and little "recovery power". In addition to retaining the shape, linings (second garment assembled independently from garment and dropped inside pants with wrong sides together) also prevent skin irritation since the fashion fabric seams are completely covered.

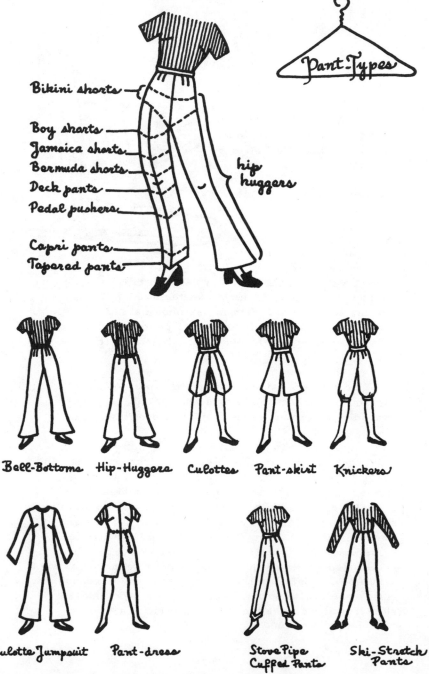

Pant-Types

Bikini shorts

Boy shorts
Jamaica shorts
Bermuda shorts
Deck pants
Pedal pushers

Capri pants
Tapered pants

hip huggers

Bell-Bottoms   Hip-Huggers   Culottes   Pant-skirt   Knickers

Culotte Jumpsuit   Pant-dress   Stove Pipe Cuffed Pants   Ski-Stretch Pants

Measuring for pants

Buy your pattern according to your hip measurement -- not waist.

To adjust the pants pattern, the pattern should equal these measurements plus suggested ease: (For a tighter fit, allow the smaller amount of ease.)

1. Waist plus 1/2" - 1".
2. Hips (fullest part) plus 1"-2".
3. Thigh circumference (taken when seated) plus 1"-2".
4. Total side seam length.

For slim pants and stretch pants, also check these measurements:

5. Length from waist to knee.
6. Knee circumference plus 1"-2" (bend knee to measure).
7. Ankle circumference plus 1"-2".
8. Over instep, across heel plus 1"-2".

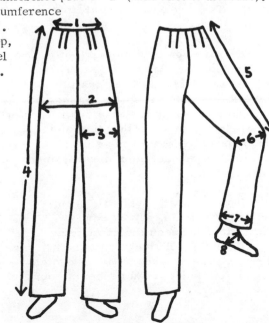

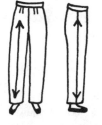

For pants to fit and hang properly, the side seams should be perpendicular to the floor, straight of grain should be down the center of the leg, and the inner leg seam should be located at mid-inner leg.

For proper fit, two crotch measurements must be taken -- depth while sitting and length while standing.

TO DETERMINE DEPTH: Sit on a hard surface (chair without cushions). For a slim figure, measure distance from waist to chair seat using a ruler (bird's eye view). For a rounded figure, measure distance from waist to chair seat using a tape measure (following curve of hips). Take measurement at side seam.

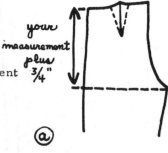

depth - SITTING

On paper pattern pieces (both front and back), draw a line across the leg from the inner leg seams (where the crotch seam and inner leg seam cross) to the side seams. The distance between this line and the waistline seam (at the side seam) should equal your measurement plus 3/4" (a).

your measurement plus 3/4"

If they aren't identical, then shorten by pinning a tuck across the pattern between the crotch and waistline (b). To lengthen, slash through pattern piece between crotch and waistline. Spread needed amount (c).

ⓐ

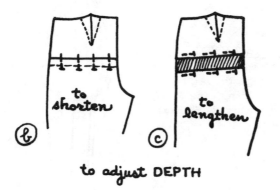

to adjust DEPTH

One big wrinkle is often found in pants (under the seat in back) when the back and front depths are not the same. (d) In joining the inner leg seams, if the back depth is more than the front, the back inner leg seam is pulled up to meet the front inner leg seam. The result: a buckling under the seat in back (e); the grainline swings toward the inner leg seam in back. (f)

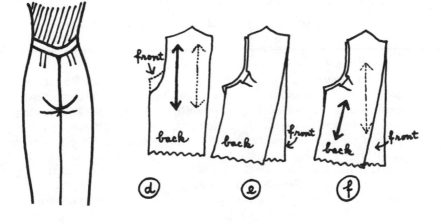

TO DETERMINE LENGTH:
Measure from waistline in
front through legs to waistline in back, holding tape
measure flat against body. (g)

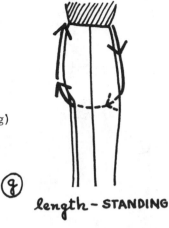

length - STANDING

    The curved stitching line at center front and center
back should equal your measurement plus ease. (h)
About 1 1/2" ease is recommended for the average
person. For a slim, petite person, this amount is
too much. For a heavier, rounded build, more ease
may be required. (To accurately measure this curved
seamline, stand the tape measure on edge so that it
follows the curve.)

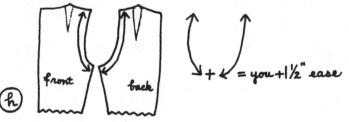

    To prevent pulling or "smiling" in either the front or
back crotch areas, locate the inner leg seam as near the
center of your inside leg as possible. For a person having
a trim figure and equally rounded in front and back, we
should be able to locate the inner leg seam in the correct
position by dividing her length in half and adding an equal
amount of ease to both the front and back halves. If the
figure is more rounded in either the front or back, then
more length must be allowed for that half of the garment.

To analyze yourself as to build, view your figure from the side. With which figure below do you identify?

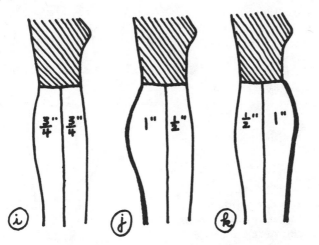

If you are equally rounded in both front and back, then divide your crotch length in half and add 3/4" ease to the front half and 3/4" to the back half. (i)

If you· are more rounded in back, divide the crotch length in half and add 1" ease to the back and only 1/2" to the front. (j)

If you are more rounded in front, divide the crotch length in half and add 1" ease to the front and only 1/2" to the back. (k)

(This amount is a suggested average. If you find the pants are too baggy with 1 1/2" ease, them eliminate some.   Or, if you are a larger person, perhaps more ease will be needed.)

The front half of your crotch length plus ease should correspond with the front crotch seamline of your pants. Add (l) to or subtract (m) from the inner leg seamline. Taper addition or reduction to the knee if a small adjustment was necessary. Taper to the ankle if more than 2" were added or subtracted.

Where a large amount is added to the inner leg seam, the thigh circumference is often too much. It is possible to remove this excess by increasing the side seams in the thigh area when the CB and CF seams are on the straight of grain. (By being on straight of grain, seams will not grow as garment is worn.) (n) Sketch center seams parallel to grain. (o) Remove same amount (that was added at center) from side to retain original waistline size. (p) Side seam will be curved.

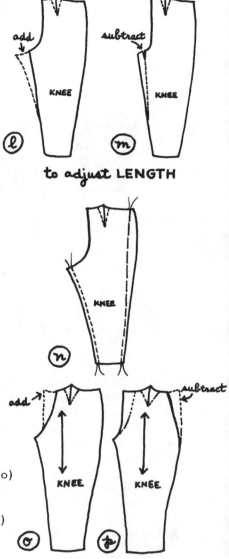

to adjust LENGTH

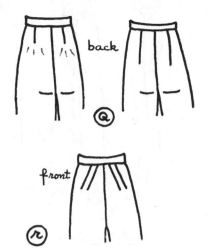

Puckers and dimples below darts in the back of pants indicate that the darts are not long enough--not extending to the fullest part of the hips. To correct: lengthen darts. (q)

Puckers in the front of pants occur with a rounded abdomen. Darts angling toward the hip bone will help the pants fit more smoothly. (r)

To stitch pants for a better fit: Seam each leg separately, stitching with grain. (s) Put one leg inside other leg to stitch crotch seam. Sew from inner leg seam to waistline in front; repeat for back. (t) Finish crotch seam like underarm seam of sleeve. Double stitch lower area, and trim seam allowance to stitching. (u)

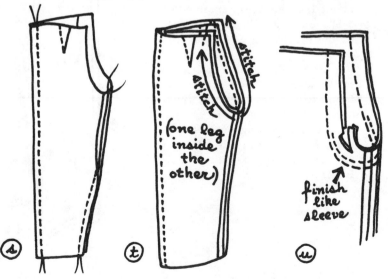

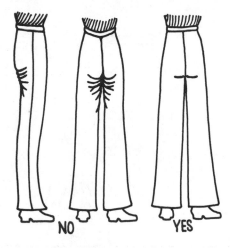

NO   YES

With correct adjustments your pants will look like the illustration on the right rather than the illustration on the left. (The left illustration shows wrinkles caused from the inner leg seam not being properly located and the back depth lower than the front depth.)

For jumpsuits and one-piece pant dresses, make crotch depth your measurement plus 1 1/4" - 1 1/2" instead of 3/4".

KNIT PANTS:

To prevent "baggy knees", cut leg front shorter than leg back. The result: slacks will stretch at the knees when sitting but will return to original position when standing because the leg was stitched under tension.

If you are under 5'3", cut leg about 1/4" shorter; from 5'4" to 5'8", cut leg 1/2" shorter; 5'9" or over, cut leg 3/4" shorter.

Stitch each leg separately to the knees. Then stretch leg front so bottom edges of front and back are together. Pin. Continue stitching seams to bottom. Refer to Elsé Patent No. 3,143,741. No license is implied.

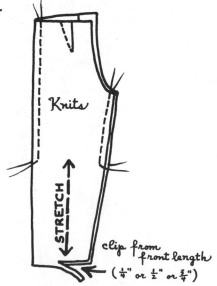

Knits

STRETCH

clip from front length (1/4" or 1/2" or 3/4")

Ski Pants

To sew your own not only means saving dollars, but you'll also have a better fit and better quality pants!

Purchase a "slim" slacks pattern, and allow the minimum amount of ease, listed on page 125. Also, make these alterations in length because the fabric will "give" in the lengthwise direction.

When buying ski pant fabric, stretch 18" to determine the amount of "give" per yard. (Ex: If 18" stretches to 21", which is 3"; then one yard would stretch 6 inches or 1 inch per 6 inches in length.) Shorten your total pant length according to the amount of stretch. (For pants 39" long, subtract 6-1/2".)

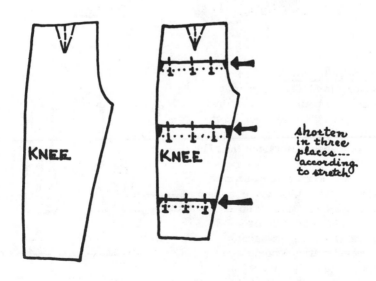

KNEE

KNEE

Shorten in three places --- according to stretch

Because the pants need to be slim at the ankle, yet large enough to go over heavy socks, a gusset must be installed in the front of the leg, (a) and a slash incorporated in the inside seam of the ankle area. (b)

For the gusset, cut a triangle of fabric 3" by 4" with stretch in the crosswise direction. Make 2" slash in front of leg. (a) Insert triangle. Spread leg so finished gusset is 3" wide at bottom. Use 2 rows of zigzag stitching to anchor.

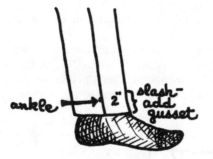 

SLASH AT ANKLE - Leave opening in inside leg seam one inch from bottom and four inches long. Press seam open. Topstitch along front edge of opening to keep seam allowance flat. (b)

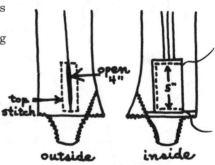

Cut rectangle of stretch fabric 2-1/2" wide and 5" long. Zigzag edges. Insert under opening. Topstitch around 3 unstitched edges of opening. Do not restitch rectangle to front edge of opening. This edge open enables pants to expand at the ankle.

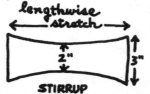

STIRRUPS -

    Cut stirrup about 4 inches long on
lengthwise stretch of fabric; 2" wide in center and 3" wide at
ends. Securely pin one side to pants at bottom edge. Try on
pants. Have someone stretch legs and pin other side of stirrup
when snug. Zigzag in place, stitching several rows.

    Either zigzag bottom edges of pants and stirrups or bind
with one inch elastic.

Stitching - Use nylon thread for all seams. Stretch seam as you
stitch if using a regular machine stitch. If using a narrow zigzag,
then it isn't necessary.

    Stitch each leg from top to bottom. Then place one leg inside
the other to stitch crotch seam. In lower crotch, stretch seam
and stitch a piece of 1/4" twill tape in seam to prevent splitting.

    Press crotch seam open. To reinforce seam and prevent
irritation, install a cotton crotch shield (similar to a dress
shield). Overlap paper pattern pieces at inner leg seam. Trace
angle of crotch. Cut 2 shields 5" long and 3" wide. Zigzag edges.
Tack to seam allowances.

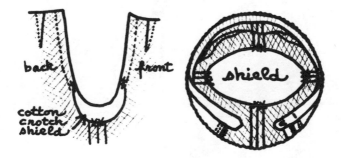

<u>Zipper</u> -

Insert an underlap extension of fabric under back half of zipper to prevent catching shirts in zipper teeth.

Install heavy trouser zipper using slot method and double stitching. Stretch seam as zipper is being stitched.

<u>Waistband</u> -

Use same principle as "grosgrain band" except use 1" elastic rather than ribbon. Stitch according to instructions on page 81. Stretch band as you stitch, or use narrow zigzag stitch.

<u>Fasteners</u> -

Use two sets of trouser fasteners, placing an eye and hook on each side of the band.

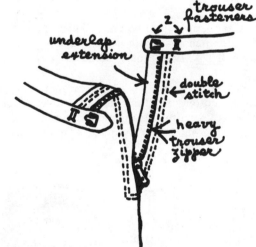

Scarves

... a necessary accessory
item for all wardrobes.

A scarf can either dress-up or dress-down a basic dress
or suit. These scarves can be made very easily by you:

1) Square scarf - Remove selvage and square fabric.
   Machine stitch 1/4" from edge -- guide for turning
   under an exact amount. Miter corners--see page
   166. Hand stitch rolled hem.

2) Self-fringed scarf - Determine desired length of
   fringe. Machine stitch where you want fringe to
   stop. Ravel fabric to stitching.

3) Attached-yarn fringe - Reinforce edges of scarf with
   interfacing where fringe will be attached. Thread
   large needle with two strands yarn. Sew through
   fabric, leaving desired length. Tie knots at edge of
   cloth to secure in position.

4) Lined long scarf - Rather than turning under the
   lengthwise edges of a scarf, either line with self
   fabric or a solid lining material. Where expensive
   silks are being used, line with lightweight lining
   (SiBonne!) to minimize cost.

INEXPENSIVE BIAS SCARF--

1. Purchase 1/4 or 1/3 yard of fabric for a scarf. For a sash or longer scarf, double the amount.

2. Seam selvage and cut edges together with one continuous seam. Begin by folding the selvage edge*to the cut edge at one end of the fabric strip. (a)

3. Begin stitching on the machine at the point you've just formed when you folded the selvage edge to the cut edge. Stitch 1/4" from the edge, stopping 1/4" from the end of the selvage. Leave the needle in the fabric and lift the presser foot.

4. Pivot the vertical cut edge to match the horizontal cut edge. Lower presser foot and continue to sew both edges together as far as possible (4-6 inches). (b)

5. Repeat above procedure until you have stitched to the end of the fabric and all edges are joined. (c)

6. Go back about to the middle and break the seam for 2 inches so scarf can be reversed. Finish opening with hand stitching. (d)
   *Fold with right sides together.

(a) fold (right side)

(b) stitch & fold again

(c) repeat

(d) break stitches → (wrong side)
Turn to inside

In most cases, you'll find a slight twist in the scarf at the middle due to making the continuous seam. Therefore, press from both ends toward the middle. (Choose solid or printed fabrics rather than plaids or stripes.)

Bias Bindings

If you are purchasing a bias binding or knit binding, then plan to stitch one or both sides by hand. It is difficult to anchor binding so that both sides can be stitched together.

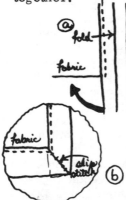

To turn corners smoothly, stitch one edge of binding to garment on right side, and as you approach the corner stitch off the fabric. Backstitch. (a)

Pivot binding to other side of corner until binding is smooth on garment and at corner. Pin in place, and hand-stitch folded edge. (b) Continue machine stitching. Anchor underside by hand.

To cut self fabric or contrasting fabric -- cut on bias* unless fabric is knit. Then cut strip in cross-wise direction as this is the most stretchy. Cut binding twice the desired width plus seam allowances. (For knits, excess bulk can be eliminated on the wrong side by leaving edge flat rather than turning it under. Attach like the Hong Kong finish, described on page 92.)

For even width, after binding has been stitched to the right side of the garment and before the back side is attached, use cardboard or magic mending tape as a guide. Turn under binding at edge of cardboard or tape that has been placed on the stitched binding.

*To save time in cutting a quantity of bias binding, follow instructions for a continuous bias strip on page 93.

Misc. Tips and Tricks

SQUARE CORNERS -- YOKES AND INSERTS:

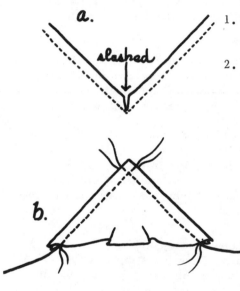

a.

slashed

b.

1. Mark point where seamlines intersect on garment. (a)

2. Staystitch garment on seam-line using small stitches, taking one stitch across point. Slash to point. (Slash will be longer than 5/8".)

3. Pin insert to garment section. Stitch with insert closest to feed dog of machine. Sew from outer edge to point; stop. DO NOT TRY TO PIVOT -- instead, tie a knot. Repeat from other outer edge. (b)

4. In order to press the seam allowance open, clip yoke seam allowance about 1" above point. Press seam open above clip. Press remaining seam allowance down. (c)

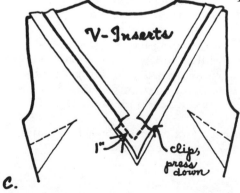

V-Inserts

1"   clip, press down

c.

CUFFS FOR BLOUSES AND DRESSES:
For a smoother look, cut both fashion fabric and interfacing on the bias rather than the straight grain.

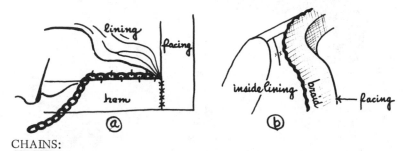

CHAINS:

Sew chain to jacket, coat or cape for additional weight to keep garment hanging in position. Stitch by hand alternating links after the lining has been installed--either at the top or bottom edge of the hem. (a)

The chain is extended from side seam to side seam unless additional weight is needed toward the front, such as in capes.

Paint the chain with clear fingernail polish to prevent the metal from discoloring light colored garments.

BRAID TRIM:

For that decorative look and custom touch, hand stitch French braid, lace or rick-rack on edge of lining where it joins facing. For interest, use contrasting colors.(b)

CIRCLE SKIRT:
For extra fullness and less stretching, cut skirt with a square waistline. Divide waist measurement by four. Cut skirt so stitchline of each quarter equals 1/4 the waist measurement. (c) Staystitch on stitching line. Clip to stitching at CF and CB points. Sew waistband in position. (For length, measure from waistline seam.) (d)

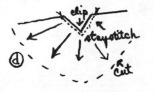

 French TACK

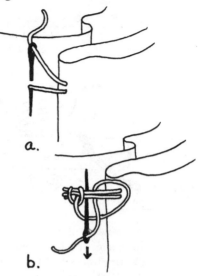

a.

b.

The French or swing tack is used to anchor two sections in an approximate position, yet permits some movement. This is done via several strands of thread, held together with a blanket stitch. Make one stitch in each section leaving about a one to two inch length of thread. (a) Use blanket stitch to hold threads together. (b)

c.

d.

e.

Suggested uses for the French tack include attaching scarves on coats (c), ties on blouses (d), and belts on dresses (e).

Another method of attaching a belt to a dress or jacket is to make a French tack on the garment (to be used as an "eye"), and attach a hook to the back side of the belt. The belt stays in place inconspicuously!

f.

DUAL PERFORMANCE:

Extend your wardrobe by obtaining two
sets of buttons for basic dresses, coats and
suits -- one set for daytime and another for
evening. It will take only a few minutes to
change to a "new and different" look. What
a space-saving idea for the woman who
travels!

REVAMP READY-TO-WEAR OR LAST YEAR'S MODELS:

That "cookie-cutter" look of mass produced garments or
"last year's model" can be eliminated by your ingenuity. Make
your wardrobe "yours"! Replace buttons and self-covered belts
with others. Add the magic of scarves, pins, chains or necklaces.

In jackets and coats, replace machine buttonholes with the
"windowpane bound buttonhole"--pages 108-111. You'll usually
find enough fabric for the buttonhole lips in the hem or facings.
Or, use contrasting fabric. Make buttonhole window slightly
larger than machine buttonhole. Or, change the shape.
Triangular, diamond-shaped or circular are all quite chic.
Merely change the shape of the window, and use wider lips.

COPY STYLES AND LINES?

It's easy with the help of a household friend--aluminum foil!
Place garment on a dress form or ironing board. Press
aluminum foil on garment. Indentations will appear at the darts
and seamlines. Add seam allowances to seam lines. Slash
dart indentations -- open darts the amount of the stitched dart.
Make paper pattern, or transfer to dress pattern, using
aluminum foil as a guide. Foil is helpful in curved and detail
areas.

SWIMSUITS:

"Swim-time" used to be summertime. However, in today's jet age, we find ourselves flying to sunny beaches in a matter of hours and swimming all year round in indoor heated pools. A "wardrobe" of swimsuits and cover-ups is not out of the question today!

Why not create that wardrobe? Because they require so little fabric and time, you can easily have several ensembles.

Whether you select a knit or woven fabric*remember that whites and pastels are usually transparent when wet. So, select an opaque fabric for underlining the suit and for the inner panty. The underlining will also prevent clinging.

If the woven fabric for the pants is cut on the bias, you'll find a smoother fit. Knits will give and conform to the body.

Preshrink everything, including elastic and zippers, since you are not allowing extra ease. When installing the zipper, plan to use an underlap similar to one used in pants (page 130), so there is no chance of catching your skin.

Buy your patterns according to bust measurements. Again, it's easier to adjust the waist and hips. The crotch length and depth will be important. To measure, see instructions under "Pants".

Interface bra section for support and shaping. Purchase a washable (woven or non-woven) interfacing. For extra support, you may want to use two thicknesses. To eliminate bulk in seams, eliminate the seam allowance on the second piece. Stitch them together and use as one. For more shaping, bra cups can be purchased and inserted.

*Permanent press and polyester blends will wrinkle the least.

For active swimming, the bra top (2-piece suit) will need some give. Buttons, used for fasteners, often "pop" off. Either stretch and stitch elastic in the side section, (a) or cover elastic for the back section. Stretch and stitch with a zigzag stitch. I generally make a loop on one side (b) and attach a garter fastener (c) on the other side. You're certain not to lose your suit in the water.

To stitch elastic to the legs, either make a casing, or enclose the elastic in the hem. Zigzag to the first fold (d), then zigzag through all thicknesses. (e)

Create an ensemble by making a cover-up from the same fabric. For extra water absorption, line it with terrycloth. (Of course, you'll need extra ease when doing this.)

And, add a 3-corner scarf or headband for that "total look".

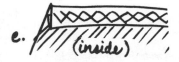

Shoulder Pads...

foundation pieces

For perfect size and fit, make your own shoulder pads. Cut a pattern by tracing around armholes--front and back. Make 4" wide at shoulders; taper to below notches on armholes. Note same grainline as garment sections. Mark with notches to distinguish which is front and back. Work on both pads simultaneously.

underlining

1. Cut a foundation of canvas and an underlining. Overlap shoulder seams; stitch. Add two more layers of canvas to foundation canvas--eliminate seam allowances making each smaller. (Canvas side will be next to garment; this will be top of pad.) Stitch.

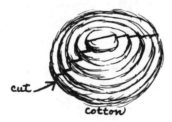

cut

cotton

2. Prepare cotton layer. Sketch a circle on paper equal to the shoulder widths and length of the pads. Pull off cotton batting; tear apart. Place it on circle to make a thin layer. Repeat, making each layer smaller in diameter and thicker at the center. Remember cotton batting will pack down!

3. Cut cotton in half--one for each pad. Place cotton on underlining, centering it over shoulder seam.

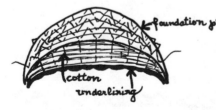

foundation pieces

cotton

underlining

4. Place foundation pieces on top. Shape over hand. Tack with long zigzag stitches (by hand) through all thicknesses.

5. Insert in garment, tacking to seam allowance or under-lining.

Tailoring

TAILORING is the construction of outer garments--coats and suits. It is a more advanced skill, yet does not have to be particularly difficult. You will be using familiar skills plus incorporating special techniques.

Special Techniques... are used because:

- the fabric is bulkier.
- the garments are worn for longer periods of time.
- the garments are usually underlined plus lined.

Advantages of Tailoring -

- individuality of design.
- exceptional fit.
- a high degree of shape retention.
- use of specific quality fabric and findings.

Jacket or Coat Terms ...used in Tailoring.

1 - fall

2 - creaseline or breakline

3 - stand

4 - notch

5 - rever

6 - lapel

7 - gorgeline

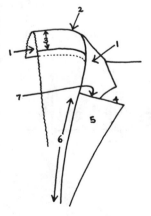

-SPEED-Tailoring

Jacket Front

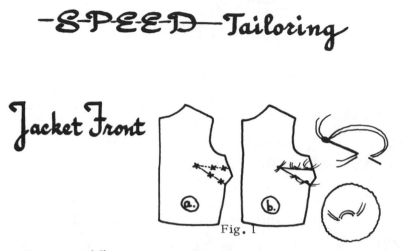

Fig. 1

1. Purchase 1/2" linen, cotton twill or rayon seam tape. Preshrink.

2. Cut underlining, fashion fabric and interfacing. Mark darts, etc. using tailor tacks for wool, (b) and tracing paper for both underlining and interfacing. (a) Fig. 1.

3. Stitch darts in underlining and fashion fabric separately. Press. Either split (a) or stagger (b) to eliminate bulk. Fig. 2.

4. Stitch dart in canvas interfacing. Cut on stitching line and remove wedge. Place a piece of bias fabric under dart; bring cut edges together over bias strip. (c) Baste. Then machine stitch or zigzag canvas to (d) bias strip. Fig. 2.

5. Press darts over ham. Let dry before moving.

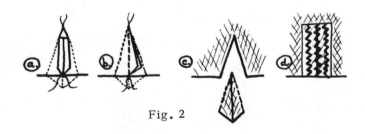

Fig. 2

Garments that button to the neck...

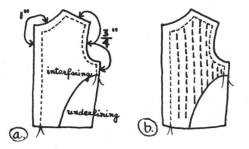

6. Place interfacing on underlining. Stitch by machine 1" from edge along front and neck. Stitch at 3/4" at shoulder, under-arm and around armholes. (a)

7. Machine or hand baste at 1-1/2" intervals throughout inter-facing/underlining piece; stitch from top to bottom, stopping 1-1/2" from bottom edge. (b) (Use 6 stitches per inch.)

8. Trim interfacing back to stitching at neck, front and underarm seams. DO NOT TRIM INTERFACING AROUND ARMHOLE. (c)

9. Tape neck (and armhole if garment is cut on bias) with seam tape or twill tape to prevent stretching. Place one edge of tape next to 5/8" stitching line. Slash and spread tape where necessary to make it lay flat; always keeping tape edge next to stitching line in tact. (d) (Tape front edge also if edge is curved--not on straight of grain.)

10. Use either straight or zigzag stitches on both edges.

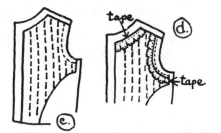

Garments with rolled lapels....

11. Place interfacing on underlining. Breakline should be marked on interfacing with diagonal line. Stitch by machine 3/4" from edge at shoulder, underarm and around armholes. Stitch one inch from edge around neck to breakline, stitch on breakline and one inch from front edge below breakline. (a)
(Interfacing will not be attached to underlining in rever area.)

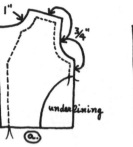 

12. Machine stitch at about 1-1/2" intervals throughout interfacing/underlining piece, stitching from top to bottom --stopping 1-1/2" from bottom edge. Stitch parallel to breakline above bustline, then parallel to center front below breakline. (b) (6 stitches/inch)

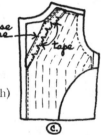

13. Trim 5/8" of interfacing from neck, front, shoulder and underarm seams. Cut diagonally at corners. Do not trim interfacing around armholes.

14. Tape neck and breakline with seam, twill or linen tape to prevent stretching. Place one edge of tape next to 5/8" stitching line around neck and next to breakline on garment side. (c) Slash and spread tape when necessary to keep flat.

15. Use either straight or zigzag stitches on both edges of tape.

FOR GARMENT THAT BUTTONS TO NECK:

16. Staystitch underlining/interfacing unit of garment to fashion fabric at almost 5/8" around the neck and at 1/2" around the other edges except the hem.

17. Follow instructions for "Underlining" --pinning and folding method--given under a separate heading.

FOR GARMENT WITH ROLLED LAPEL:

18. Staystitch underlining/interfacing unit of garment to fashion fabric. (Follow instructions for "Underlining", given under a separate heading.) Staystitch 1/2" from edge at side seam, armhole and shoulder seam; at almost 5/8" around neck; on breakline; and 1/2" from front edge below breakline. (Interfacing/underlining will not be attached to fashion fabric in rever area.) Stitch with interfacing side up.

19. Press rever using collar roll. Steam, let dry. (d) Beginning 1/4" inside breakline, pad rever*with parallel stitches by hand. Hold rever over finger as you work--to build and retain shape. (e)

20. Bound buttonholes (in the right front) would be made now.

*See page 43.

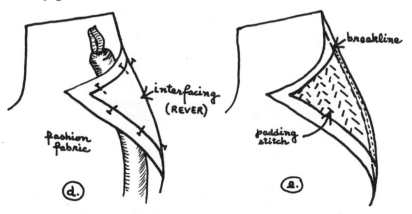

Jacket Back

1. Cut backstay from lightweight interfacing or underlining
   fabric, such as soft or firm Siri. (Since most patterns do not
   provide a pattern for this, make one by tracing around neck
   and armholes of bodice back. Make a dot
   4" to 5" below neck at center back and
   2-1/2" below armholes at side seam.
   Connect dots with curved line.)
   (a) Do not turn under

   bottom edge of backstay--leave raw edge. Center back should
   be on straight of grain.

2. Staystitch backstay to underlining 1" from neck edge and 3/4"
   from edge of shoulder, armhole and underarm. Trim seam
   allowances back to staystitching except around armhole.

3. Tape neckline and armholes following procedures given in
   "Jacket Front." Stop tape at shoulder seam line and at
   underarm seamline.

4. Attach underlining/backstay unit to fashion fabric by staystitching at almost 5/8" from neck edge and 1/2" from other
   edges except hem.

JOIN FRONT AND BACK:

Stitch shoulder and underarm seams. Press open. Trim underlining back to staystitching. Tape shoulder seam to prevent
stretching by placing seam tape flat on seam. Handstitch both
sides. Then catch-stitch seam allowance in place--to canvas in
front and backstay in back. (b)

Preparing the Collar...

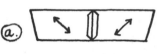

1. Join center back seams of undercollar. Press open. Trim seams
   to 3/8" tapering to 1/8" at end of
   seam. (a)

2. Trim 3/4" from outer edges of
   interfacing. Cut diagonally at
   corners to eliminate bulk.
   Trim only 5/8" from center
   back edge of interfacing. (b)

3. Tuck interfacing under center back
seam allowance of undercollar. Catchstitch. Catchstitch interfacing to undercollar around edges using large stitches. (c)

4. Machine stitch interfacing to undercollar at breakline*, using
   about 20 stitches per inch, beginning at center back and
   stitching toward each end. (d)

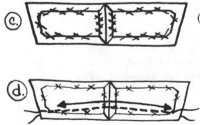

(*To find breakline on collar,
baste undercollar to garment
front and back. Where collar
rolls back is your breakline.
Mark with pins. Remove
garment and mark more
permanently.)

5. Press collar over collar roll. Continue to steam, let dry
    and repeat until collar takes roll. Use straight pins to hold
    in place. Place pins in interfacing sections. (e)

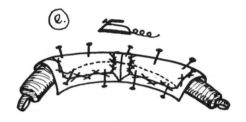

6. To pad stitch, use machine stitching (12 to 15 stitches per
    inch). Follow directions in "f", making stitches in stand
    area (next to neck) perpendicular to the breakline and stitches
    in the fall area parallel to breakline. Use either straight
    stitching or "s" stitch, such as one found on Bernina machines.
    Always stitch from center back toward each edge. Tie knots
    at each end.

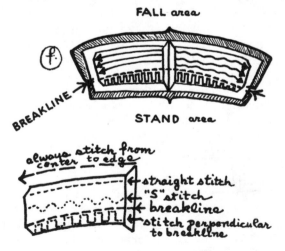

Joining undercollar and jacket

1. Stitch undercollar to jacket at neck edge, clipping to staystitching when necessary. Start at center back. Stop 5/8"
from end of collar. Clip to staystitching. (a) Trim to 3/8".

2. Press seam open. Catchstitch seam allowance on jacket side
to jacket underlining. Machine stitch collar seam allowance
to undercollar. (b)

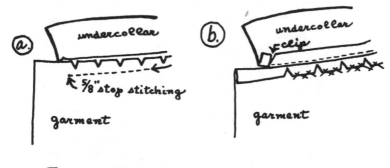

Joining upper collar and facings

1. Staystitch underlining to upper collar. (Pin and roll in crosswise direction.) Trim underlining back to staystitching.
(Stitch at almost 5/8" from edge.)

2. Underline front and back neck facings; join shoulder seams.
Press open. Trim seam allowance to 3/8".

3. Join upper collar to neck edge of facings. Clip to staystitching
when necessary. Again, start at center back and stop 5/8"
from end of collar at neck edge. (same as undercollar--a).

4. Press seam open. Trim seam allowances to 1/4". Catchstitch
upper collar seam allowance to upper collar underlining.
Machine stitch facing seam allowance to facing.

Joining collars and facings

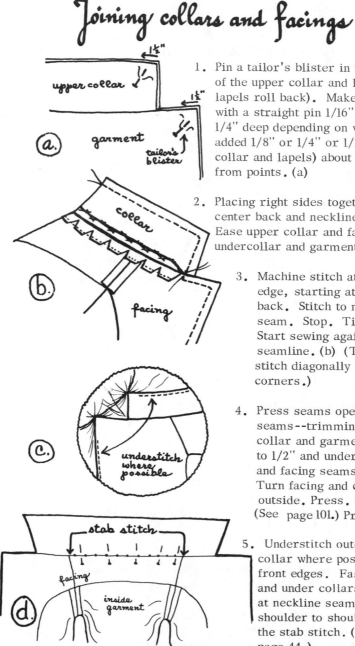

1. Pin a tailor's blister in the point of the upper collar and lapels (if lapels roll back). Make a tuck with a straight pin 1/16" or 1/8" or 1/4" deep depending on whether you added 1/8" or 1/4" or 1/2" to upper collar and lapels) about 1-1/2" back from points. (a)

2. Placing right sides together, match center back and neckline seams. Ease upper collar and facings to undercollar and garment with pins.

3. Machine stitch at 5/8" from edge, starting at center back. Stitch to neckline seam. Stop. Tie a knot. Start sewing again below seamline. (b) (Take one stitch diagonally across corners.)

4. Press seams open. Grade seams--trimming upper collar and garment seams to 1/2" and under collar and facing seams to 1/4". Turn facing and collars to outside. Press. Soap seams. (See page 101.) Press again.

5. Understitch outer edge of collar where possible and front edges. Fasten upper and under collars together at neckline seam from shoulder to shoulder using the stab stitch. (d) (See page 44.)

Finishing bottom of suit jacket

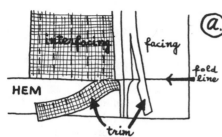

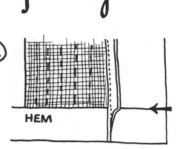

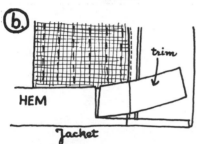

1. Cut off any interfacing that extends beyond hem foldline. Turn up hem and press. Layer side seams and front edge. (a)

2. For jacket: Trim part of hem to eliminate bulk. (b)

3. For coat: Press facings to inside. Turn back facing about one inch from fold. Slipstitch facing to garment hem. (c)

4. For jackets: Cut strip of bias interfacing 1/2" wider than hem. Place one edge adjacent to foldline.

5. Stitch bias to hem along top edge and 1/2" from fold. (d)

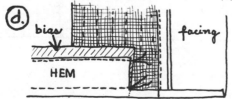

Fastening facing to interfacing

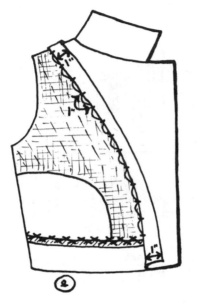

6. Fold-back facing edge about 1".
   Use long blanket stitch or half-
   feather stitch (page 43)
   and barely catch interfacing.
   Do not pull tight. Start close to
   top and end near hem. In suits,
   make stitches about 1" apart;
   in coats 1-1/2"-2" apart. (e)

7. Fasten hem to underlining.
   Fasten raw edge of facing to hem
   of jacket with tiny catch stitches;
   or turn under edge and slip stitch
   in place. (f)

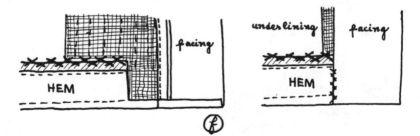

Custom Tailoring

Jacket Front

1. Purchase 1/2" linen, cotton twill or rayon seam tape, and 1/4" cotton twill tape (for taping breakline only). Preshrink on cardboard--see page 9.

2. Cut underlining (check section on "underlining" for recommended weight) for all pattern pieces except under-collar. Cut fashion fabric and interfacing. (For heavier fabrics, electric scissors are very helpful.)

3. Mark underlinings and interfacings only.

4. Pin underlining to front, back, facings and upper collar using "pin and fold" method. (See section on "underlining".) Do not join hair canvas to front or undercollar yet.

5. Before staystitching underlining to fashion fabric in garment sections having darts, baste (6 stitches per inch) through center of dart from point to wide end--starting one inch beyond point--to hold two fabrics together. (1)

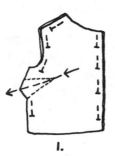

1.

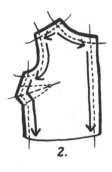

2.

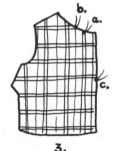

3.

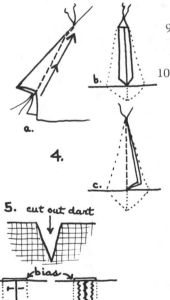

4.

5. cut out dart

6. Staystitch (12 stitches per inch)
   curved neckline and lapel area at
   5/8" from edge; staystitch 1/2"
   from other edges except bottom.
   (Wait until ready to turn up hem
   to sew across bottom edge of
   jacket and sleeve.) (2)

7. Transfer markings from underlining to right side of fabric via
   contrasting thread. (Mark center
   front; buttonholes; collar point--a;
   top lapel point--b; and bottom lapel
   point--c.) (3)

(To determine roll in collar and lapel--
baste collar to jacket. Mark where collar
rolls back on you. This is your breakline.)

8. Stitch darts in bodice from wide end
   to point catching only one thread for
   the last three stitches. (a)

9. Press darts; either split (b) or
   trim (c) to eliminate bulk. (4)

10. Prepare dart in canvas interfacing
    by cutting on stitching lines and
    removing wedge. Place a piece
    of bias under dart; bring cut
    edges together over center of bias
    strip. Baste canvas to bias strip.
    Then machine stitch in zigzag or
    zigzag pattern. (5)
    (Bias strip serves as buffer
    between interfacing and fashion
    fabric. It also keeps interfacing
    dart in tact.)

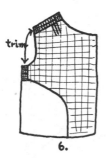

6.

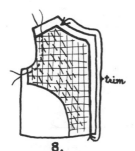

7.

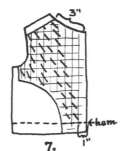

8.

9.

11. Pin interfacing to jacket front with bias strip of dart next to underlining. Trim shoulder and underarm seam allowance from hair canvas. (6)

12. Tailor baste*hair canvas to underlining beginning 1" from front edge at hem of jacket and ending 3" from front edge at top of jacket. (7) (Cloth should be smooth over canvas.)

13. Baste at seamline around armhole to anchor interfacing to fashion fabric. (8)

14. Trim front edge of interfacing back along front and neck edges so it is 3/4" from edge of fashion fabric. ·Cut diagonally across point to eliminate bulk. (8)

Padding lapels

15. a. Mark collar point and two lapel points on canvas. Draw diagonal line connecting lapel points. (9)

   b. Machine stitch (20 stitches per inch) through jacket and interfacing on this breakline.

*See page 44.

c. Shape lapel using collar roll..
Steam, let dry. Hold lapel in
place with straight pins. Do not
remove collar roll until dry. (10)

d. Beginning 1/4" inside breakline,
pad*rever with parallel stitches.
(These should barely catch wool.)
Hold rever over hand as you work
to retain rolled shape. (Single
strand silk or waxed cotton threads
are best to use. Beeswax prevents
tangling.) (11)

*See page 43.

Taping Front Edge

16 a. Pin tape (1/2" width) to interfacing
so one edge is at 5/8" stitching
line of front edge and neckline.
Begin at bottom, make square
corner at rever tip. Slash and
spread or slash and overlap tape
around curved edges. (Always
slash from inside edge of tape to
keep edge in tact at seamline.)
(12)

b. Fell stitch*to interfacing. Stop
at shoulder seamline.

*See page 43.

Taping Break Line

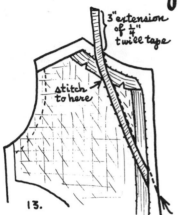

3" extension of 1/4" twill tape

stitch to here

13.

17 a. Pin piece of 1/4" twill tape
tautly next to breakline
(with tape toward body
section of jacket). For
small bust, pull tape 1/8"-
1/4" tighter; for large bust,
pull tape 3/8"-1/2" tighter.
(This keeps jacket lapel area
closer to chest--thus eliminating
the gap in this area.)

b. Fell stitch in place, stopping
at edge of neck tape.

c. Leave 3" extension on tape--
when collar is attached, this
tape will be stitched along
breakline in collar for extra
support. (13)

(Bound buttonholes would be made now in
right front.)

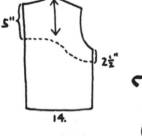

5"   **2½"**

14.

Jacket Back

1. Underline fashion fabric. Stitch
shoulder darts.

2. Apply backstay to shoulder area to
give extra support. (14)
To cut, see instructions on page 152.

3. Tape back neck edge like front,
beginning and ending at shoulder
seam. (15)

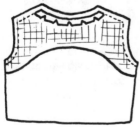

15.

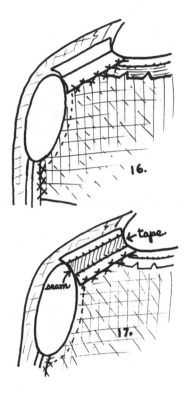

4. Join underarm seams of front and back. Press open.

5. Stitch shoulder seams; press open. Trim under-lining and backstay seam allowances to staystitching.

6. Tuck front interfacing under seam allowance. Catchstitch front shoulder seam allowance and under-arm seam allowance to canvas. (16)

7. Tape shoulder seam by placing 1/2" tape flat on top of stitching line. Fell-stitch*both sides. (This prevents shoulder from stretching.) (17)

*See page 43.

Preparing Collar

1. Join center back seams of undercollar. Press open. Trim to 1/4", tapering to 1/8" at end of seam. (18)

19.

2. Trim 3/4" from outer
   edges of interfacing.
   Cut diagonally at corners
   to eliminate bulk. Trim
   5/8" seam allowance
   from center back of
   interfacing--tuck under
   center back seam allowance
   of undercollar. Catch-
   stitch in place. (19)

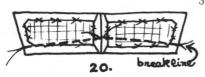

20.   breakline

3. Machine stitch interfacing
   to undercollar at breakline,
   beginning at center back
   and stitching toward outside edge. (All stitching
   on undercollar will be
   done from center back
   toward outside edge--so
   both sides look alike.)
   (20)

21.

4. Shape collar over collar
   roll. Hold in place using
   straight pins. (21)
   (Steam and let dry.)

5. Pad collar by hand making stitching perpendicular to breakline
   in stand area. In fall area, make rows of stitches parallel.
   (Work from center back toward each side.) (22)

6. Steam press over collar roll again.

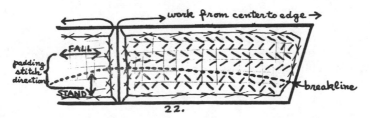

→ work from center to edge →

FALL

padding
stitch
direction

STAND

← breakline

22.

7. Remove 5/8" wedge from each corner of neck edge of
   undercollar. (23)

8. Miter both outside corners on undercollar. (23) Cut diagonally
   at corner 1/4" beyond stitching line. (24-a) Fold back that
   1/4" and press. (24-b) Turn under two adjacent seam
   allowances. Press.

9. Trim to 1/4" and machine stitch seam allowances to undercollar. (24-c and 25)

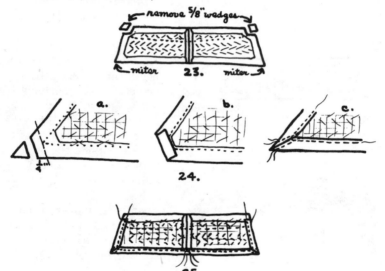

10. Staystitch underlining to upper collar. (Pin and fold in
    crosswise direction.) Trim underlining back to staystitching.

11. Remove 5/8" wedge from each corner of neck edge of upper
    collar, like undercollar. (See previous section and
    illustrations.)

12. Miter both outside corners on uppercollar.

13. Instead of machine stitching seam allowance to uppercollar,
    use the catch-stitch. Stitch to underlining only.

PREPARE LAPELS AND NECKLINE FOR COLLARS:

1. Underline front and neck facings.

2. Join front and neck facings at shoulder. Press seams open. Trim underlining to staystitching, and trim this seam allowance to 3/8".

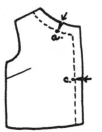

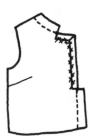

26.

3. Trim underlining to staystitching along front and neck edges of jacket and along front and neck edges of facings.

4. On facings and bodice, slash to seamline at collar point and bottom lapel point. ("a" and "c" in 26)

5. Miter corner; turn under seam allowance between points "a" and "c". Trim seam allowance to 1/4" on garment, 1/2" on facing. Catchstitch to underlining. (27)

27.

Attaching Collar

1. Clip curved neck edge of facing to staystitching. Stitch upper collar to facing neck edge. Press seams open; Trim to 1/2". Catchstitch to underlining. (28)

2. Clip curved neck edge of garment to staystitching. Stitch under collar to garment neck edge. Press seams open. Trim seams to 1/4". Machine stitch collar seam allowance to collar. Catchstitch garment seam allowance to garment underlining. (29)

28.

29.

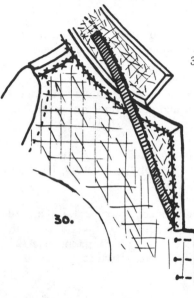

30.

3. Stitch seam tape extension along collar breakline-- with tape on stand side of undercollar. One edge of tape should be next to breakline. Either machine or hand stitch. (30)

4. Pin jacket to jacket facings, right sides together, below lapel area. Stitch. (30)

5. Trim seam allowance of facing to 1/2"; jacket to 1/4". Press seam open. Turn back facing; press. Soap seam*allowance. Press.

6. Understitch, stopping at hem fold. (31)

*See page 101.

31.

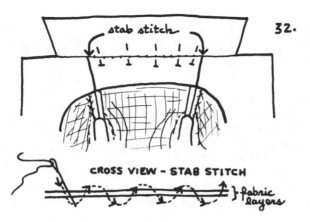

7. Stab stitch*upper and under collars together at neckline seam from shoulder to shoulder. (32)

8. With wrong sides together, ease upper collar and lapel to undercollar and underlapel. Pin from upper side. (To make joining easier, use tailor's blisher at points.) Pin tuck about 1-1/2" back from points. (33) Make a tuck with a straight pin 1/16" or 1/8" or 1/4" deep depending on the amounts the upper collar and rever were enlarged.

9. Fell stitch collars together. When tailor's blister is removed after stitching is completed, tuck automatically means bubble in upper collar--so collar points will turn under.

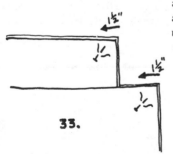

Finishing bottom edge of garment - see pages 157-158.

Fastening facing to inter-facing - see pages 157-158.

*See page 44.

Man's Jacket ... interfacing

In a man's jacket more firmness in the chest area is desired.
Three layers of interfacing are
used to create this firmness. A
man's jacket features a creased
breakline rather than a rolled
lapel and collar. Select a rayon/
cotton canvas or linen canvas rather than a hair canvas.

1. Cut the first interfacing (Formite) like that for a woman's
    jacket. Extend interfacing under armhole. (a-1)
2. Top with a second piece 12"-14" in length, cut with grain-
    line parallel to creaseline. Place 1/2" back from the
    creaseline. (a-2)
3. Cut a third piece of lightweight wool, felt or underlining
    about 11"-12" in length and 1" less in width than the second
    piece of canvas. Superimpose on second piece with edge
    again located about 1/2" from creaseline. (b-3)
4. Either machine stitch or tailor baste through all thick-
    nesses. (c) Tape front edge, edges of layer #2, and
    creaseline. Use 1" twill tape for creaseline so edges of
    two layers will be covered. Machine stitch. Place tape at
    front edge 5/8" from edge of jacket.

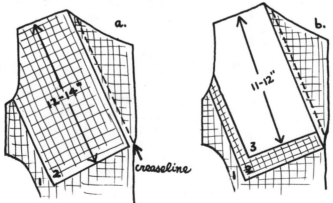

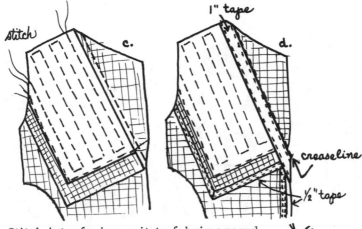

5. Stitch interfacing unit to fabric around neck, down creaseline, at front edge, shoulder, under arm and around armhole. Pad stitch rever. (e)

6. Pad collar using either machine stitch (p. 153-154) or by hand (p. 165). To eliminate bulk and use machine stitching, select lining fabric for undercollar.

7. To attach collars, follow directions on p. 155-156.

8. For outside chest pocket, cut rectangle from inter-interfacing section to eliminate bulk.

(For quick, easy pockets, follow pocket adaptation of windowpane buttonhole on page 111.)

9. Finish hem following instructions for the defined hem on p. 88. For vent, fold on hem and catchstitch. (Trim part of hem from inside vent.) Slipstitch bottom edges. (f)

10. (The jacket back and sleeves would be constructed like the woman's jacket.) Shoulder pads are needed. Hand baste in position before lining jacket.

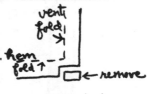

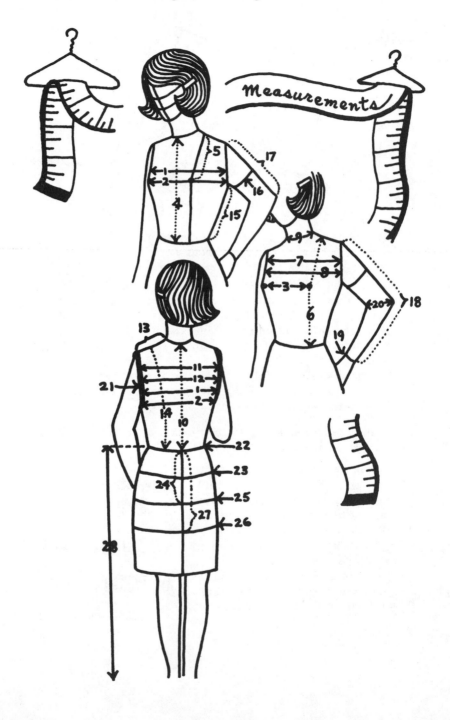

TAKING MEASUREMENTS:

1. Wear proper foundation garments--those you plan to wear with the garment.
2. When measuring thighs for slim skirts or slacks, measure while seated.
3. Use cloth or fiberglas measuring tapes--those do not stretch.
4. For accuracy, have another person take your measurements.
5. Record measurements every six months.

BODICE:

1. High bust --
   - front half   _____
   -back half   _____
2. Full bust --
   - front half   _____
   - back half   _____
3. Bust point to bust point _____
4. Center front bodice length_____
5. Length - shoulder to bust point_____
6. Length - shoulder over bust to waist_____
7. Chest width, (2" below neck at CF) armhole to armhole _____
8. Chest width, (4" below neck at CF) armhole to armhole _____
9. Neck circumference _____
10. Center back bodice length (from prominent bone at neck to waist) _____
11. Back shoulder width (4" down) armhole to armhole _____
12. Back shoulder width (6" down) armhole to armhole_____
13. Shoulder length, neck to arm socket --
   Right _____
   Left _____
14. Length, center of shoulder over shoulder blades to waist _____
15. Underarm bodice seam, armhole to waist _____

SLEEVES:

16. Upper arm circumference (point where sleeve joins garment at underarm) _____
17. Arm length, shoulder to elbow _____
18. Arm length, shoulder to wrist _____
19. Wrist circumference _____
20. Elbow circumference (bend arm) _____
21. Sleeveless armhole: front half _____
                             back half _____
    Set-in sleeve armhole: front half _____
                             back half _____

SKIRT:

22. Waist _____
        front half _____
        back half _____
23. High hips (3" down) _____
24. Waist to fullest part of hips _____
25. Full hips _____
        front half _____
        back half _____
26. Thighs (taken while seated) _____
27. Waist to thighs _____
28. Skirt length, waist to floor --
            front _____
            back _____
            left side _____
            right side _____

AVOID "MARK-DOWNS" WITH PROPER FIT

No matter how many years you've been sewing or whose pattern you're using, it's the appearance on you that makes the difference.   You can look like "a million dollars"--designed and made especially for you, or like you "borrowed" from your neighbor or "bought a sale item just because it was marked down".

The way your clothing fits is important to appearance and comfort. Even though construction may be superior in quality, without a perfect fit that garment will not have a smart, fashionable look.

This alteration and fitting section is geared to help you understand the principles of altering patterns and fitting garments. This actually involved balancing the grain of the cloth and removing wrinkles by either adding or subtracting in certain areas. Most alterations should and can be made in the paper pattern before the fashion fabric is cut.

BUYING PATTERNS

Patterns vary in both size and type. Check both before buying:

SIZES vary in measurements while TYPES vary in proportions of the figure. TYPES include: girls, misses, womans, half-sizes, etc. The same size in two figure types may have the same bust, waist and hip measurement but differ in height and bust position. Also, there are differences in length of shoulder seams, depth of armholes, position and depth of bust darts and the waist length.

Determine your figure type by comparing your height, back waist length and bust position with figure type and measurement charts.

To determine your size, compare your measurements with the ones for your figure type. Find the size having measurements closest to yours. If you fall between two sizes--select the smaller size if you're small boned, and the larger one if your bone structure is large.

Use bust measurement when buying patterns for blouses, coats, dresses and suits. (Since the upper chest area is most difficult to adjust, purchase a pattern that fits that part of the body rather than the hips!). If your full bust measurement is between two sizes and your high bust measurement corresponds with the smaller size, buy this size and increase the full bust area.

Buy patterns for slacks, shorts and slim skirts by hip measurement...not waist measurement. Use waist measurement for gathered or dirndl skirts.

NEW SIZING

The New Sizing, introduced in 1967, was adopted by the major pattern companies to bring pattern sizing closer to standard ready-to-wear sizing. This does not mean that they will always correspond exactly. Therefore, it is necessary to measure yourself carefully and buy a pattern that corresponds with your measurements.

Even though there are standardized measurements, the amount of ease (wiggle room) varies between patterns and companies. The ease varies with the styles, the fabrics, the designers, and the size.

Add ease to your personal measurements for a comfortable fitting garment. Or measure a garment which you feel fits well and record those measurements. Below I am listing minimum recommended ease for the major areas of measurement: (A person with a larger bone structure and build would possibly want more ease.)

Full bust	2-1/2" for blouses and dresses; 4" for suit jackets; 5" for coats.
Waist	1" for fitted garments; more for princess styles & shifts.
Hips & thighs	2"

Back shoulder width (4" below neck at center back, from armhole to arm-hole)	1/2" for sleeveless garments; 1" for set-in sleeves; 1-1/2" for coats.
Wrist	1/2"-1" for slim fitting sleeves.
Upper arm circumference (arm measurement where sleeve sets into armhole)	2-1/2" for dresses, blouses; 4-1/2" for jackets; 5-1/2" for coats.

PERMANENT PATTERN

Once your basic shift, bodice, skirt and sleeve pattern are adjusted, make them "permanent". Press "iron-on" interfacing on the back of the paper pattern piece. Then use these patterns to check the new patterns you buy. (It's more time-saving than using a tape measure.) Place new tissue pattern on top of permanent pattern to check bust, shoulders, waist, hips, etc. You can easily see where alterations should be made.

Pattern Adjustments

for skirt

...LENGTH --

Change at bottom for slim skirts. For shaped skirts (A-line, circle), change within pattern so bottom stays same size.

SLIM

SHAPED ← make changes here

↕ make changes here

...INCREASE - DECREASE HIPS --

For 2" or less, change hips at side seam. (a) For more than 2" totally, slash from bottom to top, but not through waistline, and toward side seam where width is needed (ex: 9" below waist). Add same amount at bottom of skirt as added to hips. Redraw bottom edge to straighten. (b) (Without the horizontal slash, more inches would be added to the bottom edge than the hips, thus changing the shape of the skirt.)

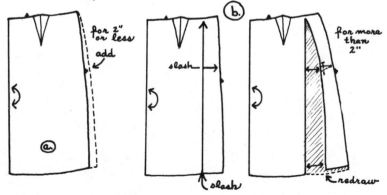

for 2" or less add

(b.)

slash →

for more than 2"

(a)

↓ slash

↘ redraw

...INCREASE - DECREASE WAIST --

For 2" or less, adjust waistline at side seams. (a)

For more than 2", slash from the waist to the side seam between the dart and seam. Open at waistline. Redraw cutting line by connecting edge of slash and outside seam edge. (b)

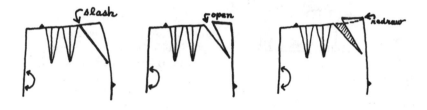

...GAPPING PLEATS --

For the box pleat that gaps, lift inside section of pleat at waistline until edges come together.

...PROMINENT OR FLAT DERRIERE OR ABDOMEN --

Symptoms: Prominent--garment is shorter at CB or CF.
Crosswise grain is not parallel to floor. (a)
Flat--garment is too long at CF or CB, and there is extra
fullness below the darts. (b)

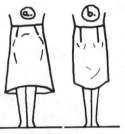

1. Slash paper pattern piece from
   center to outer edge about 4-5
   inches below waist, and pin waist
   line of pattern to you. (Wear a
   full length slip.)

2. Spread or overlap pattern needed
   amount until crosswise grain is
   parallel to floor. (c) Straighten
   center front or back seam lines.

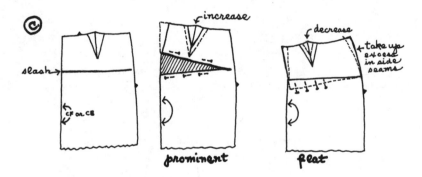

3. Increase darts at waistline for prominent abdomen or
   derriere; for flat, decrease size of darts, taking up extra
   in side seams.

...SWAY-BACK --

Symptoms: side seams of skirt swing forward; and extra fabric at waistline in CB area.

For correction, lift skirt at CB until side seams are perpendicular to floor. This amount should be removed at CB waistline.

For skirts, pin tuck from CB toward side seams, tapering to nothing. (Lowering waistline will add inches there.)

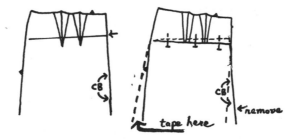

For a one-piece shift, slash or pin tuck from CB toward side seam at wasitline. Fold or overlap needed amount.

Using yardstick, straighten CB grainline. Align yardstick with CB of bodice. Trim excess from skirt area. (Otherwise, you'll have a tail!)

Tape this trimmed amount to side seam to maintain the correct number of inches at bottom edge. (Otherwise, skirt will cup at hem.)

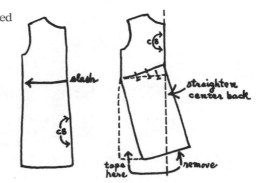

for bodice

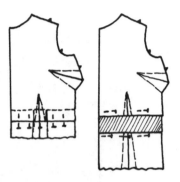

...LENGTHEN OR SHORTEN --

Draw a line across pattern below bust dart. Slash and spread pattern pieces the needed amount to lengthen. Form a pleat to shorten length.

The same procedure would be used for a one-piece shift dress or coat.

Reconstruct darts by connecting waistline dots and point.

...LENGTHEN OR SHORTEN AT CENTER FRONT OR CENTER BACK ONLY --

If it's necessary to adjust the length only at center front or center back, then slash from the center to the side seam edge below the bust dart. Spread or overlap the needed amount.

Straighten the center edge, and redraw the vertical darts so they are parallel to the center.

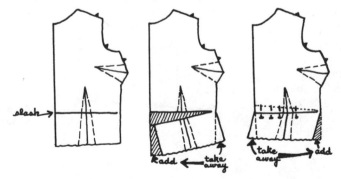

If length was added, straighten the center edge by using a yardstick. Remove from the side seam the same amount that was added at the center.

If the pattern was shortened, then remove excess from the center, and add it to the side seam (so waistline is the correct size).

Reconstruct the dart angle by lengthening the center of the dart line from the point down. At the base or waistline, make dart the same size as on the pattern.

...INCREASE - DECREASE BUSTLINE --

Determine bust point by drawing a line through center of both bust and waistline darts. Where lines intersect or cross is the bust point.

Slash pattern through center of waistline dart to bust point and toward armhole edge. Slash through center of bust dart to bust point. Spread pattern at bustline the needed amount (1/2 actual amount needed to increase since pattern is usually cut on fold). Do not add to waistline. As bust area is being increased, bust dart will also open, thus keeping the pattern flat. And, if an increase is needed in the bust, a larger dart could also be used.

Redraw point of waistline and bust darts to stop 1" outside bust point. Sew bust dart using original lines.

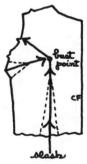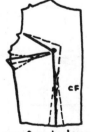

slash   spread to increase   overlap to decrease

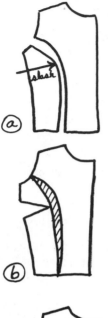

...INCREASE BUSTLINE OF PRINCESS STYLES--

Locate bustpoint by using tape measure from shoulder to bust point. Slash side panel from cutting edge to cutting edge toward bust-point. (a)

Overlap stitching lines on both panels at waistline and shoulder or armhole. At the same time, spread the panels at bustline so space between panels equals amount needed. Tape to tissue. As panels were spread apart, the bustline dart automatically opens. (b)

Cut panels apart along cutting line of front panel--tissue is added to side panel. Close and tape side dart so pattern looks like the original one! (c)

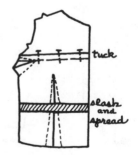

...RAISE-LOWER DARTS --

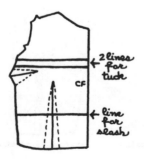

Rather than re-drawing actual dart--

To raise--draw two parallel lines between dart and armhole
--distance equals amount to raise. Form tuck. Tape.
Below dart, slash across pattern and spread same amount
as tuck. Pattern is again its original length.

To lower--draw a line between dart and armhole--spread
open the amount dart needs to be dropped. Draw two
parallel lines below dart--distance equals amount spread
above dart. Form tuck. Tape.

...NARROW CHEST --

Symptoms: excess fullness above bustline.

Make an "L-shaped" slash through shoulder and side seams.
Remove section. Slash horizontally toward armhole about
4" below shoulder--not through armhole.

Overlap "L" section the needed amount across chest and at
shoulder. Horizontal slash toward armhole enables you to
subtract different amount at lower and shoulder edges.

Redraw underarm seam.

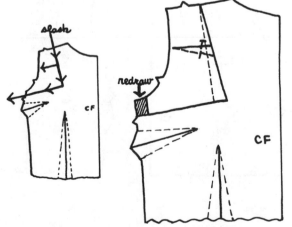

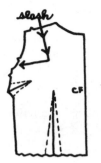

...SHOULDER WIDTH --

Make an "L-shaped" slash in the pattern through the shoulder and to the armhole edge. For narrow shoulders, overlap needed amount at shoulder. Redraw shoulder seamline.

For broad shoulders, spread needed amount. Redraw shoulder seam, again matching outer edges.

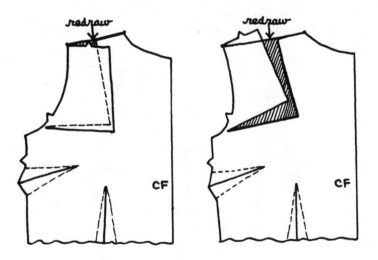

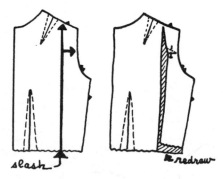

...UPPER BACK WIDTH --

Slash pattern from bottom
to top between darts and
armhole. Slash horizontally
to armhole where extra width
is needed (4"-5"-6" down
from neck edge at CB).

Spread needed amount
adding no extra width to the
top and bottom edges.

Redraw bottom edge of pattern connecting outside and slashed edge.

For a narrow back, overlap instead.

...PROTRUDING SHOULDER BLADE --

Slash from bottom to top, but not through shoulder completely.
Slash between darts and center back. Slash horizontally to
armhole where extra is needed. Also slash from neckline
toward vertical slash.

Spread needed amount in blade area. Pin together shoulder
dart, thus throwing open new dart at neckline. Mark new
dart using cut edges of pattern as outside points. Draw a
new point about 3" down slash.

Redraw bottom edge if necessary, connecting outside edge
and slashed edge by dart. And, redraw waistline dart so it
is parallel with the center back.

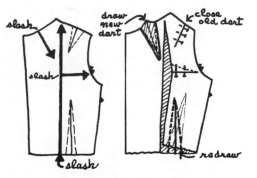

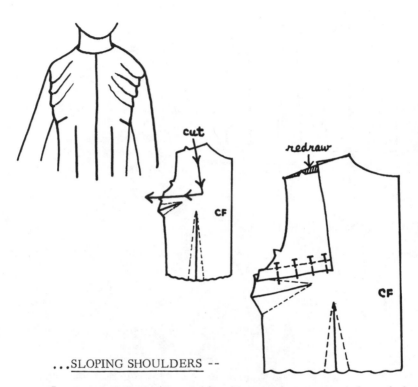

...SLOPING SHOULDERS --

Symptoms: diagonal wrinkles from neck area toward armholes
indicating too much fabric in outer shoulder area.

Again, make an "L-shaped" slash through center of shoulder
and across pattern between armhole and bust dart.

Overlap armhole piece the amount needed to eliminate
wrinkles. Redraw shoulder seam connecting outer edges of
seam.

(Note--no change has been made in the size of the armhole.
If the excess length had been removed in the shoulder seam,
the armhole would be too small and binding.)

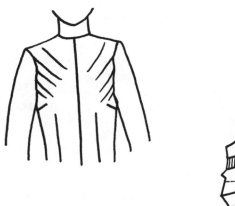

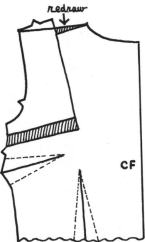

...SQUARE SHOULDERS --

Symptoms: diagonal wrinkles from center area toward
shoulder area indicating a pull on the fabric.

Make an "L-shaped" cut through center of shoulder and
across pattern between armhole and bust dart.

Lift armhole piece the amount needed to eliminate wrinkles.
Insert paper. Redraw shoulder seam, connecting two outer
edges. (Note--no change has been made in the size of the
armhole.)

... ROUND SHOULDERS --

Symptoms: diagonal wrinkles in back only from neck toward armholes. Also, crosswise grain is not parallel with floor at 4" below neck, and bottom edge of blouse or jacket is not parallel with floor.

Slash pattern from CB to armhole about 4" below neckline at CB. Also, slash through shoulder dart to, but not through horizontal slash.

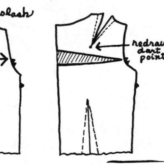

Spread pattern the needed amount. Shoulder dart will open automatically to keep pattern flat. Use dart's original lines for stitching. Redraw point of dart.

...SCOOP NECK THAT GAPS --

A slash is made from the neck to the bust point and through the waistline dart to its point. Overlap the neckline slash and tape. This will open and increase the waistline dart size. Use original lines for stitching.

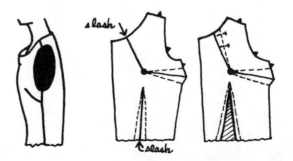

GAPPING NECKLINE IN BACK --

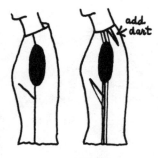

Usually the neckline gaps because there is no dart or it is too small.

Add a dart to the neckline, tapering toward the shoulder blades. Also, remove the same amount from the facing and collar neck edges.

WRINKLING BELOW NECKLINE IN BACK--

This means the garment is too long at center back and in the shoulder area.

Make neck deeper at the center. Increase width of shoulder seams, and add darts at the neck.

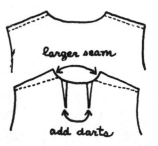

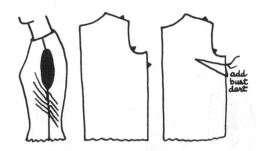

NO BUSTLINE DARTS:

Some patterns today have no bustline darts. If a stretchy
or clinging fabric (jersey) is used with no underlining or lining,
then the garment looks fine. However, when a woven material is
used and the woman is full through the bustline, she'll find
diagonal wrinkles under the arm, and the dress could bind. In
that case, add a dart. Transfer one from another pattern that
fits. Add to the front bodice side seam length so it is the same
as the back.

BUCKLING AT THE ARMHOLE:

Buckling at the armhole is eliminated by making the
bustline dart larger. Rip upper side seam of muslin. Smooth
fabric on person around armhole. Include excess fabric in
dart--upper side of dart. Add to the front bodice side seam
length so it is the same as the back. Otherwise, the armhole
will be too large.

Eliminating Side Seams

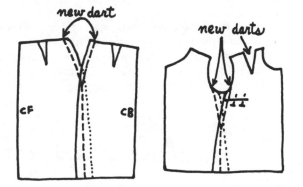

When working with fashion fabrics that require matching (plaids) or are difficult to press (velvets, leather), eliminate side seams when possible.

For a slim skirt, overlap side seam allowances near the bottom of the garment. The remainder of the seam will be stitched in the form of a dart.

For a blouse, dress or vest, transfer the underarm dart to the shoulder. See instructions on pages 27-28. Then overlap side seams of garment. Stitch the remainder of the seam in a dart.

Irregular Figure

Since most people are the same size on both left and right sides, making the same adjustment for both sides would be correct. However, if your left and right body halves are not the same, then it is necessary to make a pattern for the entire front or back rather than cutting it on the fold.

Muslins – trial garments

bathrobe and coat   for beach or dress

Before cutting expensive fabrics, make a trial garment to double check pattern adjustments. Many classes suggest unbleached muslin. It's good; however, most of these muslins become "dust rags". Why not use housecoat fabric when testing a coat pattern? And terrycloth (beach jacket) when testing a jacket? Your time and energy will be spent on a garment you can wear rather than throw away. And, at the same time, you've checked your pattern!

For slacks, do not use muslin. Instead, select a firmly woven broadcloth.

1. A garment fits well when it adapts itself to the wearer's body, accents good features and skillfully hides poor ones.

2. The factors that contribute to good fit are so interrelated that if one is incorrect, the others will be affected.

3. These lines are considered in judging fit: shoulder, armseye, neck, waist and hemline. The location of these lines varies with fashion.

4. Lengthwise grain or lines should be vertical at center front and center back--perpendicular to the floor. In the basic set-in sleeve, the lengthwise grain hangs perpendicular to the floor from the tip of the shoulder to the elbow.

5. Crosswise grain should appear horizontal (parallel to floor) at the waist, across the bustline, upper back, hips, sleeve cap (about 4-1/2" below shoulder), and hemline.

6. Bustline darts should point to the bust, but stop one inch before the bust point. To find the bust point on a paper pattern, draw lines through the center of the bustline and waist darts. Where the two lines cross is the bust point.

7. Single sleeve darts in long sleeves should be at the elbow. With triple darts, the middle dart is at the elbow. And, with double darts, the elbow is between them.

Sewing for Children

Because children have a way of "growing like weeds", we must take into consideration "growth features". These features and tips will extend the life span of garments for children:

1. Choose firmly woven or knit fabrics.

2. Select garments having raglan sleeves--no set-in sleeves.

3. Add cuffs on sleeves that can be unfolded for length. Add length to ready-to-wear by adding cuffs of contrasting color or knit cuffs.

4. Make hems extra wide; incorporate hair canvas to prevent the fold crease from showing and to reduce abrasion on that fold. (See page 89 -- "Softer Rolled Hems".)

5. Choose garments without waistline seams. However, if there is a waistline, ease fabric to elastic rather than seam tape. The dress can then stretch and expand as the child grows.

6. Make a tuck under the belt or sash--the width of the belt. For additional length, the tuck can be released. The belt covers the "let-down" area and camouflages any color fading.

7. Incorporate outside bias facings at the neckline of the dress in contrasting color. When length is needed, add bias (same width as facing) to hem edge.

8. Have jumpers button at shoulders. Leave extra length on each strap.

9. To cover wear lines (folds) on hem when dropped, use braids, rick rack and trims. Add also to sleeves, collars, etc. to tie garment together.

10. Use elastic casings at waist for waistbands on skirts and slacks.

11. Velcro fasteners on outer garments let children dress themselves.

12. Make a double breasted coat with raglan sleeves larger by moving over buttons to make it single breasted.

13. For a dress-up outer garment, a cape or poncho can be worn for a longer period of time due to extra width across chest and shoulders and no sleeve length. Make it reversible for even more mileage.

14. Wear extra-short dresses over pants as tunics.

15. Have vests fasten at both sides. Allow an extra amount on the underlap side so buttons can be moved over as the child grows.

Leather ~ Suede ~ Vinyl

Because needle holes and pins stay in these materials, stitching must not be removed, and pins should only be used in the seam allowances. Therefore, it is imperative to fit a garment before it is stitched.

Rather than basting the leather pieces together, baste and fit the underlining. Remove basting. Sew *underlining to leather, suede or vinyl. All these need to be underlined because of their tendency to "stretch". *(Do not backstitch. Tie knots.)

To cut: Do not cut pieces on the fold. Make a pattern for the entire front, etc. Place pieces on the right side of the leather with all pieces either going the lengthwise or crosswise direction. Eliminate bulk by cutting garment with 3/8" seam allowances. Mark on the wrong side with chalk or pencil. Or, mark underlining with tracing paper. Use lining fabric for facings to eliminate bulk. (Select patterns with simple lines and few darts.)

Press seams open using a warm, dry iron and brown paper as a "press cloth". On curved seams, cut small "v's" from the seam allowances. Tap seams open with a hammer. Spread a thin line of fabric glue or rubber cement over stitches on both sides of seam line. Use clapper as a weight until glue dries. Topstitching will also keep seams open. Or, use flat-felled seams instead. Overlap seams on stitching lines; topstitch twice.

This is SEWING?

To hem: Do not stitch. Glue in position.

buttonholes

For buttonholes, use "windowpane" bound buttonholes (pages 108-111) in soft leather. Just cut rectangle in garment and facing--1/4" wide and length of buttonhole. Slip lips between two layers of leather. Topstitch around window to hold lips in place. For heavier skins, slash and stitch twice around edge of slash.

With vinyls it may be necessary to use waxed or tissue paper, glycerine or baby powder on the surface to help it move evenly through the sewing machine.

Permanent Press

Garments made with permanent press fabrics are marvelous timesavers in the laundry department. However, in the sewing department they can cause head-aches if special techniques are not used.

Fabrics with this finish are "set" or "cured" before being sold over the counter. You'll find it impossible to straighten the yarns, and, in many cases, remove the crease for the center fold. If you can't press it out, then it's not going to come out. So, lay out pattern pieces around the fold--avoiding it.

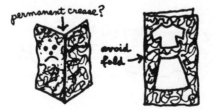

permanent crease?

avoid fold →

Select patterns with the least amount of seaming since it will be difficult to press seams flat. Consider topstitching to keep seams flat. Check the section on "Sleeves" for the correct amount of ease in set-in sleeves before cutting. (See page 54.)

Use polyester thread and permanent-press interfacings. Staystitch curved areas at 5/8" from edge rather than the conventional 1/2". Don't forget to preshrink zippers and trims.

Crepe

Many women are frightened when they think about using crepe.

You'll recognize crepes by their pebbly feel. You've also seen the word "crepon". This is not a true crepe. It's pebbly surface is acquired by running a heated roller over the fabric's surface. They're used frequently for coat and jacket linings, dresses, blouses and pants.

Crepes are available in almost every fiber -- "plain or bonded". Here are some suggestions for the plain crepe:

Because crepe is soft, it could cause problems when cutting and sewing. First, select a simple style with few pieces. In cutting, you'll find it "moves" on "slick" surfaces such as a formica table top. So, cover your cutting table, or use a cardboard cutting board for accuracy.

crepe "moves"

In sewing, it will be necessary to pin frequently and even use tissue paper under the crepe. In stitching, use polyester thread for polyester crepe; silk thread for wool crepe; mercerized cotton for rayon crepe. Hand-pick zippers. (Nylon zippers would be best because the cloth is lightweight.)

Press seams open using the seam board (page 103). This will prevent the seam indentation from showing on the right side.

Underline garments for extra support.

Bondeds

Bonded fabrics are here to stay! The garment manufacturing industry finds them invaluable -- easy to cut and sew, and they look good on the hangers. How they look after being worn is another story!!! Most bonded fabrics are either loosely woven or knit cloths fused to a knit tricot. Because the tricot and adhesives give extra body (firmness), the fabric manufacturer can eliminate many yarns per inch in both crosswise and length-wise directions. These fabrics give and stretch out of shape. (The sad part is that many won't recover and go back to their original shape when cleaned and pressed. Consequently, we have a "sagging back" or "rump spring" problem.)

Again, I repeat from pages 17 and 18, it is essential to underline and line these fabrics if you want a professional look!

Personally, if I could choose between a woven cloth and a bonded cloth for the same price per yard, I'd choose the woven cloth. You're getting a better buy--more yarns (and many times higher quality yarns) per inch.

Many of the bonded fabrics are finished off grain and can't be straightened. Check before buying. Don't buy fabric that is off grain.

bonded?

Interface all edges and details for extra support. Machine made buttonholes rather than bound buttonholes wear better due to the open weaves and loose knits used in bonded fabrics. For coats and jackets, use a buttonhole substitute (p. 112-118).

Because of construction of the cloth, most bondeds do not ravel. Pinking the edges would be sufficient.

Eliminate excess ease at the cap of a sleeve for a smoother look (p. 54).

Knits

You're searching for a wrinkle-
free, easy-care wardrobe?
Then knits are the answer.
They're hard to surpass for every-
day use and travelling.

The weight of the fabric and the garment's style will
help you determine whether to line or underline. (See p.
17-18.) For a clinging look, use light-weight knits.
For soft control, underline with tricot. Select
simple styles with few details and seams. To
keep seams flat and prevent curling, make
narrow seams and zigzag edges together. (a)

Interface necklines, collars and hems. Use permanent-
press interfacing (Armo-Press) for polyester, nylon and
triacetate knits used in blouses, dresses and pants. For
jackets and coats use a washable hair canvas (Acro). To
prevent curling of facing edges on lighter weight, slinky
knits, interface the facing rather than the neckline and
zigzag edges together. (c) For an unlined garment, stitch
pre-shrunk seam or twill tape in shoulder and waistline
seams, "v" necklines or inserts to prevent stretching.(b)

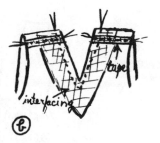

Eliminate bulk by using lining
for undercollars and facings.
(See page 68 for the faced
facing.) For any knit you plan
to launder, process all fabrics
and notions so all will perform
the same. This permits knit to
relax, also.

Polyester thread or **fine** lingerie thread is suggested for knits as it will give with the fabric and prevent puckered seams and popped seams. A stretchy thread means a straight stitch can be used. Zigzag stitches are only needed where **thread** doesn't stretch or where garment stretches extensively (swim-suits, ski pants, girdles). A stretch-stitch on your machine can also be used for these fabrics.

Staystitch and interface seams before installing zipper. Cut 1" strip of inter-facing on the bias. Stitch 1/2" from edge and zigzag edges together. (d) Install zipper by hand or machine. To eliminate bulk at waistline seam for zipper installation, slash seam about 1 1/2" from center-back edge. Press open. (e)

For smooth set-in sleeves, adjust ease at cap of sleeve according to page 54.

Eliminate the bulky look at the waistline (f) when heavier double knits are used. Stitch preshrunk seam tape to waistline seam over gathers. (g) Also, eliminate some fabric by cutting notches from gathered edge. The result--a trim and slim looking waistline! (h)

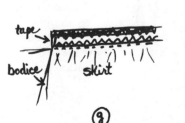

Conclusion

Sewing is an art like gourmet cooking! Most anyone can fry an egg, but to take that egg and fluff it into an omelette is something else again. To serve that egg a la Benedict is yet another step! Sewing the straight seam may not be so exciting. But to consider fabric, tension and pressing tricks on the straight seam or to turn that seam around a scallop, point it at the lapel or shape it into a sleeve for the desired effect is the challenge. Increasing skill increases satisfaction, and the effort becomes an art.

Sewing is a universal activity. A look at what is sewn, how it is sewn tells some truths about the people and their place. In some areas sewing is a way of life. In some, it is a necessity. With some people it is a discipline, but with others it is simple pleasure. From crude peasant embroidery to the finest tailoring, sewing is a creative experience in spite of the motivation for taking the needle and thread in hand.

In our culture people sew because they are interested. Their wants may stem from some needs, it is true...like making children's clothing last longer or providing items for special figure problems. But mostly sewing is done because someone wants better looking, better made clothes than the same amount of money could buy; or a high fashion look at low budget figure;

or a unique custom-created garment. They sew because it's fun! They sew because it's the thing to do. It is the proud and fascinating leisure time effort of women of all walks of life--and of some men, too. Sewing is at once challenging and simple, and therefore appealing to a variety of age groups.

But not everyone sews equally well. Training and knowledge are important. Happily, sewing is a skill one can acquire rather than a gift that comes at birth like a wish from the good fairy. Learning to sew beautifully is a most valuable pursuit.

"A job worth doing is worth doing well" is a time-worn adage that applies to sewing. A garment poorly constructed looks "home made" and won't bring the desired raves. The hand made look with couturier quality is what today's seamstress is striving to reach. Doing the right thing in the right way helps. There are new ways of doing old things and better ways of doing obvious things which skilled artisans and technicians of the sewing field have evolved. These make the difference.

In this book the latest and best methods have been set forth in an understandable manner to enlighten the experienced sewer and instruct the novice **so she, too, can create professional** looking garments. High fashion sewing is now within the reach of you, the reader.

210